Richard Paul Evans

◆

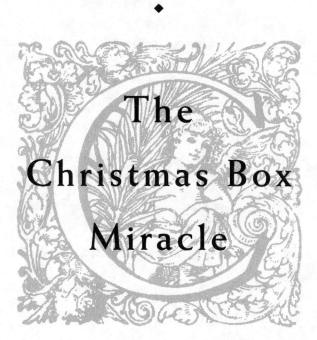

The
Christmas Box
Miracle

My Spiritual Journey of
Destiny, Healing and Hope

◆

SIMON & SCHUSTER
New York London Toronto Sydney Singapore

SIMON & SCHUSTER
Rockefeller Center
1230 Avenue of the Americas
New York, NY 10020

SIMON & SCHUSTER and colophon are registered trademarks
of Simon & Schuster, Inc.

Book design by Ellen R. Sasahara, based on design by Pei Loi Koay

Manufactured in the United States of America

ISBN 0-7432-1942-2

Acknowledgments

◆

I WOULD LIKE TO THANK the following for their support and assistance on this book. David Rosenthal for the suggestion that it was the right time for this book. Carolyn Reidy for continued support and interest in my works. My always magnificent editor, Sydny Miner. Laurie Liss, part of the journey. Isolde Sauer. (Consider this an early Christmas present.) Brandi Anderson for research and enthusiasm. The crew: Lisa May (midwife to the angels), Tawna Spoor, Becky Avery, Judy Schiffman, and Jed and Fran Platt. I also thank my former neighbor, Susie Gardner, for her suggestion to publish *The Christmas Box.* And Clark Yospe, who not only encouraged me to publish but called a publisher. And Sexton Paul Byron who gave the angel its first home.

Of course, my sweetheart Keri and the tribe. We will miss you, Krista.

Thank you to my loyal readers around the world. I love you and appreciate your loyalty and encouragement.

*To God, the source of all
destiny, healing and hope*

◆

Contents

◆

CONTENTS

When I was twenty-four years old I attended a lecture by one of the great scientific minds of our generation—a man who has been compared to Copernicus, Galileo and Einstein—the British physicist Stephen Hawking. During the lecture Professor Hawking posed a question to the audience that seemed to trouble him. Why, he asked, given the relativity of time, can we remember the past but not the future?

I have puzzled over his query for some time. And I have wondered if there are those who can indeed remember the future. Maybe that's how my grandfather knew. Maybe that's why he told me when I was still a small boy that the Christmas Box Miracle would happen to me one day.

—*Richard Paul Evans*

The
Christmas Box
Miracle

What I Believe

◆

*T*HIS BOOK IS ABOUT FORCES that move about us like wind—unseen, yet powerful enough at times to knock us over. And it's about a little Christmas tale I wrote that was the result of such forces. Some call these forces divinity, others call them coincidence. Some just call them magic.

A few years back a newspaper reporter was interviewing me about the miraculous story behind my story *The Christmas Box*. Near the end of the interview he said, "You don't really expect me to believe all this."

I wasn't surprised by his skepticism. I wouldn't believe most of it myself if it hadn't happened to me. "I suspect you'll believe what you want to believe," I said. "Start with what you can see. A twenty-nine-year-old man from Utah, having never before written a book, with no publishing experience, no knowledge of the book industry and very little money, writes his first book, publishes it himself and for eight weeks outsells the biggest authors and publishing houses in the world."

He thought for a moment, then said, "Your explanation makes more sense."

◆

As a novelist I find it ironic that this story, the most unlikely of my books, is the only one that is true. Yet, as unlikely as it may be, the miracle of *The Christmas Box* is undeniable. According to the *Wall Street Journal*, *The Christmas Box* had one of the highest one-week sales of any book in its list's history (until Harry Potter came along). It is the only book to simultaneously hit number one on the *New York Times* hardcover and paperback bestseller lists and the only novel to hit number one as a self-published book. *USA Today* listed it among the top twenty bestselling books of the last half decade.

But more incredible are the stories I encountered along the journey—miraculous stories of healing and curious coincidence that often defy explanation. These are experiences that have changed the way I view the world.

In telling these stories I will try not to editorialize too much. (Just the facts, ma'am.) I will leave it to you to interpret their meaning. Still, like the reporter, in the end you will believe what you will. Ironically, the opening words of *The Christmas Box* are perhaps even more relevant to this book:

> *I share my story now for all future generations to accept or dismiss as seems them good. As for me, I believe. And it is, after all, my story.*

◆

Through the course of my Christmas Box journey there are eight things I have come to believe.

First, to paraphrase Shakespeare, I believe there is more to heaven and earth than is dreamt of in most people's philosophy. I believe there is occasional interaction between our world and the unseen world. I believe the gift to me of *The Christmas Box* was such an interaction.

Not that I have desired such gifts. Outside of prayer, I have never sought contact with the unseen world. I've never talked to a palm reader, sat in a séance or had my tea leaves read. I've never had the slightest desire to call the Psychic Friends Hotline.

Shortly after *The Christmas Box* hit the bestseller lists and it became known that I claimed my story was a spiritual gift, New Age disciples grilled me intensively on "channeling"—the phenomenon of communicating with spirits. I was not interested in the discussion. I don't know how *The Christmas Box* story came to me. It just did—as if it were whispered to my mind.

The media sometimes makes light of my assertion of "divine assistance," yet I'm far from being alone in such claims. Even Robert Louis Stevenson claimed that fairies delivered his stories. My feelings on this matter are similar to author Stephen King's, who once told a reporter who doubted his explanation of where his stories came from, That was fine, as long as he believed that King believed it.

I'm not surprised by the media's skepticism. I'm likewise doubtful of most of the stories I hear of supernatural phenomena, and dismiss 99 percent of them as fanciful. It's the other 1 percent that gives me pause.

For instance, I was speaking to a large group at a professional women's conference. It was a good speech, if I say so myself. The room was packed. The words flowed. I received a standing ovation. Afterward I was ushered out to sign books at a table in the hallway. Standing in the line was a woman, sharply dressed and well groomed, with an air of poise and self-confidence. And she was visibly shaken.

"I can't believe what I saw," she said, half whispering to me, afraid that someone else might hear her. "Has anyone else told you they saw something unusual while you were speaking today?"

I told her that I didn't know what she was talking about.

She glanced about nervously. "I can't believe everyone in the audience didn't see it. While you were speaking there was suddenly a young woman standing next to you." She looked me in the eyes. "You didn't see the woman next to you?"

"No."

Her forehead wrinkled. "I've never seen anything like this. I don't know what to make of it. It's like something out of *The Twilight Zone.*" With that she walked away.

I didn't know this woman from Eve. Maybe she just escaped from the high-security ward of the local mental hospital, but I doubt it. First, because the mentally ill embrace their delusions, not question them. Second, because in spite of her agitation, she spoke reasonably. She acted precisely the way I would act if I saw something I couldn't explain. I don't know what this woman saw, if indeed anything. But from what I know of human behavior, I believe that *she* really believes she saw something.

Then again, maybe she was playing some twisted sort of prank, in secret conspiracy with a minister in Denver, an aspiring author in Maui and all the other people in other parts of the world who have told me *precisely the same thing*— that they saw a young woman standing next to me as I spoke. I've never seen this young woman they speak of. Maybe she exists, maybe she doesn't. I'm not sure that I care. It's the phenomenon of perfect strangers making the same claim that intrigues me.

◆

Second, I believe there are specific moments in each life given us to influence our life paths—a cosmic pull of a lever that switches the tracks beneath us. History abounds in such "accidents." Like the trip to the city when Henry Ford happened to come across a motorized vehicle. Like Thomas Edison's saving the life of a telegraph operator's son and being given a job at the telegraph office, where he created his first invention, or Eli Whitney's chance meeting of the widow Catherine Green and her suggestion that he might invent a machine to separate cotton from its seeds. If such providence is evident in the lives of the great, then why not the rest of us?

Third, I do not believe we are some accident of God or nature. I believe there's a purpose to our being here on this earth, and the experiences that we have come to us for our own spiritual growth and evolution. Earth is about learning, and the day it stops, school is over. Maybe that's what Heaven is—an extended summer vacation. Or more likely, a chance to use what we learned about being human. Perhaps we might have even agreed, in some premortal state, to the experiences and trials we face.

I was in Tulsa, Oklahoma, on a book tour, eating dinner with my media escort and her husband, when I shared with them a few of the miracles I describe in this book. When I finished, they both were quiet. Then the woman said, "We believe you. We believe there's a divinity to our lives. You need to tell the world what you've told us. We need to know there's a reason we're here."

I agree. I believe it's vital that we know of our *divine life purpose*. Not just to hold on to as a frightened child clutches its blanket in the darkness of her bedroom—this is about more than easing our loneliness and fear in an apparently silent void of a universe (though it may have that effect).

Only in understanding and accepting our *divine life purpose* can we view the world as it really is and free ourselves from the pursuit of the "perfect life" as painted by Madison Avenue and other paradigm engineers, and pursue instead the *perfect life experience*—a divine education—so we can evolve as spiritual beings.

I believe this is among our greatest quests in life, not just to see life as it really is but to see our part in it.

Fourth, I believe that as we pursue our *divine life purpose*, spiritual forces will intervene to give us the experiences we need. To quote Shakespeare, "There's a divinity that shapes our ends, rough-hew them how we will." Call it, if you will, God's "micromanagement" of our lives. This, perhaps, is the very crux of this book—to document a few of the hundreds of experiences that have led me to believe in such divinity. As I wrote in *The Looking Glass,*

While the mathematics of the universe may connote the existence of a Supreme Being, to me it is that which defies math's probabilities—the impossibility of two objects colliding in an infinite void to alter each other's eternal course. In this there is divinity and an unseen hand. Perhaps this best describes my concept of God—the divine, unseen wind that propels us through the uncharted waters of our own destiny.

Such interference may be a major, life-changing event, or as simple as an experience I had a few years back in San Diego. It was before I had a publisher, so I was driving myself from a book signing, navigating a rental car on unfamiliar roads in the dark, looking for my hotel. I was lost, lonely, hungry and tired. I was also discouraged, as the book signing had been a failure.

Suddenly I had the powerful impression that I should pull off the road into a parking lot. I followed the prompting. As I pulled in, I noticed a bookstore that I hadn't seen from the street. I thought that it must be why I had the impression. For some reason, I thought, I needed to visit *that* store. I found a parking place and put the car in park. Immediately there was a knock at my window. I turned to see a woman standing outside. She was young, dressed in tattered clothing. Two small children huddled behind her. I cracked open my door.

"Excuse me, sir," she said, "my children are hungry. I was wondering if you could feed them tonight."

I looked at the children, who hid their faces from me in their mother's coat.

"Of course," I said.

Across the parking lot from us was a Jack in the Box drive-in. That night I ate dinner with Mary, Angel and Bobby.

Fifth, I believe that in order to fulfill our life purpose it is vital that we ask for divine assistance in our lives. There is tremendous power in desire, and the unseen powers of divinity that can affect our lives are oftentimes just waiting for us to ask for their aid. I believe these forces must wait for our request because they are bound by the law of free agency and cannot intervene in our lives until we exercise our will and ask them to.

For instance, many years ago I had the desire to visit China. Though I didn't have the financial means for such an excursion, I wrote down my desire and prayed for the opportunity. Then, unintentionally, I forgot about the goal. Six months later a friend of mine called out of the blue. She was a media buyer and had just won a trip for two to China. She wanted to know if my wife and I would accept the trip from her as a gift. It was a life-changing experience for us, as years later, influenced by our trip, we adopted a little girl from China.

The biblical injunction "Ask and it shall be given" is paraphrased in nearly every religious text I have studied. I learned early in life about the power and efficacy of prayer. I believe that the miracles in this book would not have been possible had I not first asked for them. That which we ask of life is indeed all that it can ever be.

Sixth, life is not a solitary affair and was never meant to be. On our individual journeys there are companions placed along the trail, fellow sojourners who forever alter our paths and help determine our destination. Sometimes they carry us when we are too weary to carry ourselves. In retrospect, it is evident to me that throughout the Christmas Box Miracle there were people who stepped in at the right place and right time to carry the miracle forward. Without them this book would never exist.

Seventh, I believe that preceding each personal and spiritual victory there must be a moment of adversity—a literal trial of spirit. These dark times, when many fall with despair, are the real moments of triumph. I need not cite more than Winston Churchill's magnificent speech: "Let us therefore brace ourselves to our duties, and so bear ourselves that, if the British Empire and its Commonwealth last for a thousand years, men will still say, 'This was their finest hour.' "

For everyone who strives for success, there must come such a time. The greatest moments of most endeavors are not usually caught on film or applauded by large, adoring crowds. These are the trophies, not the victories. They are not the same thing.

The greatest moment of the Christmas Box miracle was not the day my book became a number-one bestseller. The greatest moment (as you will read) was a deeply personal and solitary triumph of spirit—a battle waged in no more spectacular a place than a shopping mall parking lot without another soul in sight.

Remembering that each noble cause must be preceded by a struggle enables us to better walk with courage and faith.

Eighth, I believe the most important thing that we can learn in our divine educational process is *how to love.* To love God and to love others. They are the same thing, really. We cannot love God without loving his children. Neither can we love God without serving his children.

A few summers ago I took my oldest daughter, Jenna, on a humanitarian mission into the jungles of Peru. After a few days of hiking and sightseeing, crocodile hunting and dining on piranha (it tastes like chicken), we set up a clinic in the jungle. Our group consisted of about twenty volunteers, mostly college students, along with two optometrists and one dentist.

My job at the clinic was to assist the eye doctors by

searching through suitcases filled with used eyeglasses in an attempt to match the doctors' prescriptions. Jenna, along with another teenager, used hand puppets to teach the Quechuan natives about hygiene and sanitary practices. She also helped watch the children while their parents were being seen by the doctors.

A week and a half later, Jenna and I sat with our backpacks in the Lima airport waiting for our flight home.

"What did you learn from this?" I asked Jenna.

She said she wanted to think about it. About twelve hours later we were sitting in Chicago's O'Hare Airport when I noticed that Jenna was crying. I asked her what was wrong.

"Dad, we have so much and they have so little." Then she said something I will never forget. "I know what I've learned," she said. "We love those whom we serve."

My teenager got it. Love without service is as dead as faith without works. It is only in reaching beyond ourselves to save others that we save ourselves. As Victor Frankl, a psychiatrist and a Jewish survivor of the Nazi concentration camps, wrote in his book *Man's Search for Meaning*, "I grasped the meaning of the greatest secret that human poetry and human thought and belief have to impart: The salvation of man is through love and in love."

Love is oftentimes most beautifully rendered on canvases of travail. Like the men Frankl wrote about who, despite their own starvation, shared their crusts of bread. Or like Jesus on the cross.

In relating my story, my hope is that you might see not just my journey but the possibility of your own. It may be your first step in achieving all that you desire from your life. And your own greatest destiny.

1

◆

GIFTS

$\mathcal{M}$Y GRANDFATHER HAD what Christians call "gifts of the spirit." Grandpa Evans was a serious man, devout in his religious beliefs and conservative in dress and speech. Still, at least to me, there was a discernible energy in his presence. Many said that he could, at times, work miracles. As a child I witnessed some of those miracles. None, perhaps, was more evident than the one I saw after my brother Van was electrocuted.

I was nine years old. It was the same year our family moved to Utah, leaving behind the beautiful, palm-tree–lined streets of Arcadia, California, a suburb to the east of Pasadena.

Arcadia lived up to its name. It was a childhood Eden, lush and innocent, the kind of place where a child should grow up. Peacocks freely roamed our neighborhood, as did we children. It's no wonder "Arcadia" pops up frequently in my books.

Things were good for our family there. My father was the administrator of a large chain of convalescent hospitals and my mother never worried about money in those days, except that we might have too much and that it might spoil us. I remember once asking my mother if we were rich.

"We're rich because we have the gospel," she replied.

"But are we *rich?*" I asked, hoping for a better answer. She frowned and turned away.

◆

We had a large two-story house with a heated swimming pool, surrounded by a brick terrace and ornamental kumquat trees and a water fountain with a Greek-style statue. My father drove a brand new Buick Riviera. We had a pet capuchin monkey named Tony that could chirp happily like a bird and bite like a vampire. We went on frequent family outings, often to Long Beach or Disneyland or whatever particular amusement my mother and father conceived of for the weekend.

In spite of our money, my mother, as thrifty as she was pious, sewed many of our clothes. For one of our family outings she made us matching pink-and-olive shirts, which to my teenage brothers' and sister's horror, we wore in public. It was Mom's way of keeping track of all eight of us. We looked as wholesome as a sixties Tide commercial. As a kid I thought all this was great. But this was in the tie-dye and bell-bottom culture of the sixties, and to this day I'm surprised that my teenage sister, Heidi, ever came out of the house.

I was the seventh of eight children in a Mormon family, the sixth of seven boys. I suppose ours was typical of large family culture; a pecking order existed, easily understood by even the youngest of us: big fish eat smaller fish. My parents told me that my first uttered sentence was, "Help, Mom, Dad. Help." This came at just two years of age, as my older brothers hung me over the stair railing by my feet.

My older brothers spent much of their time devising tortures for us younger ones. One Christmas, one of us kids received a large cloth tube made for crawling through. The older brothers threw it into the swimming pool, then made us younger children swim through it. Their idea of fun was to close off the ends of the tube, forcing us to hold our breaths and swim back and forth until we looked really desperate. Only then would they open one of the ends.

When my second-oldest brother, Scott, bought his first motorcycle, influenced by the antics of Evel Knievel, he immediately began to jump it. First he jumped small wooden ramps, then dirt hills. Then he jumped us. I remember lying on my back and watching the motorcycle sail over me. His best was sixteen feet and three brothers.

I'm not sure why we never defied *the brothers*. Perhaps we realized that resistance was futile. With a family as large as ours, unless we were bleeding, an appeal to our mother was nothing more than a guarantee for future retaliation from our older brothers. More likely we were just fools. The older brothers were cool and we wanted to be part of their world. If lying beneath a flying motorcycle was what it took, so be it. It's a wonder that any of us younger children survived childhood.

Just two months before my fourteenth birthday my father lost his job and, with promise of employment, we sold our home and migrated to the warmer and more prosperous climate of southern California.

THE CHRISTMAS BOX

In the spring of 1969 my father lost his job. Slowly our Camelot crumbled. My father sent résumés out by the ream, but without success. With a family as large as ours to provide for, things quickly turned desperate. When, after nearly a year of unemployment, he was finally offered a job at Idaho State University, in Pocatello, he took the position. Packing up the Buick, he drove to Idaho with Heidi and Mark, while my mother and the rest of us stayed behind in California to sell the house.

Though we missed our father, we were glad that Mark was gone. Mark was the third son and our most feared tormentor. He used more imagination in devising our tortures. One of his originals was to come upon us as we slept, slip an empty plastic milk jug over our hand, then tickle our face. He would also sit on our chest (this was torture enough, we thought), then pour honey on our face and call the dog.

It should be noted here that later in life Mark became my intellectual hero. He speaks seven languages and helped engender my love for literature, convincing me to read dead authors with just three words, "Chicks dig Shakespeare."

At this time my oldest brother, Dave Jr., now the man of the house, convened a family council. We younger children respected Dave. First, he was six feet tall, which was about a mile taller than the rest of us. Second, he had little interest in torturing us. He was old by our standards, seventeen, and he had discovered girls and the Doors and had better things to do with his time than waste it with the affairs of children.

Dave had taken an empty pickle jar and told us that we needed to fill it with money so that our mother could afford the gas to drive to Idaho to see our father. Everything we could earn was to go into that jar. Dave worked tirelessly, mowing lawns and doing odd jobs for neighbors. At a time when he might have been using his money for dating, all of his earnings went into the jar. I was not so noble. I remember raking leaves at a neighbor's home and receiving thirty-five cents for an hour of work. When I got home, I wrestled with sacrificing my precious coins to the jar. Nobility lost. I never put the money into the jar. In truth my offering was never even missed, but I had not done my part, and even though I was only eight at the time, I still feel shame when I think of it.

When the house finally sold, my parents decided that a small town like Pocatello would not afford their children the opportunities they should have in life. My father quit his job and we moved together to Salt Lake City to live in the dilapidated house my mother's mother had left vacant by her death.

In truth, the pea green wood-shingled structure was anything but vacant. It was rat infested from its peeling tile floors to its mildewed ceilings. At night Van and I, lying shoulder to shoulder in the same bed, would pull the covers over our heads and listen to the rats scurrying beneath and above us. The movie *Willard* was big at that time, a peculiar horror film about a boy whose best friend was a rat, the leader of a pack of rats that went around eating everyone who was mean to the kid.

Though Van and I were too young to see such a movie, our older brothers had seen it and regurgitated it to us in all its gory detail. Then, reveling in our terror, they garnished their telling with scenes from George Orwell's *1984*, Upton Sinclair's *The Jungle* and any other literature that evoked flesh-eating mammals.

Van and I were mortally afraid of rats. I remember one night lying awake in bed for hours, trapped beneath the sheets by fear. I desperately needed to use the bathroom, but didn't dare leave the bed as I was certain that the moment I touched my foot to the cold tile floor, I would be set upon by piranhalike rodents intent on stripping the flesh from the bones of small boys. I don't recall the outcome of that night, though I'm sure it wasn't pretty.

◆

We had left Los Angeles during the height of social upheaval—when the *L.A. Times* headlined violent anti–Vietnam War demonstrations and university riots, LSD injected into milk cartons and razor blades found in Halloween candy. "The world has turned wicked," my mother told us. "These are the last days." Even at the age of eight, I remember that there were things we were to fear.

We children believed that Utah was to be a haven of sorts. A land of milk and congeniality, where everyone was kind and neighbors waved to one another from across the street. We couldn't have been more mistaken. We had moved into one of Salt Lake's inner-city neighborhoods, just a few blocks from the pawnshops and beer joints of State Street. My first weeks in Utah I learned that my hair and my pants were too short. I learned to fight and the meaning of several four-letter words I had never even heard before.

I remember one of our first Saturday mornings in Utah. My mother drove us down to see the kids' movie at the

Avalon theater, a mile from our home. The Avalon still exists, though it now shows only old black-and-white films for a dollar and hosts the Amazing Maxwell the Hypnotist on weekends.

As the three of us—my brother Van (who was two years my senior but not much bigger than I), my little brother Barry and myself—walked out of the movie, we were followed by a group of children. One of the older boys had picked the three of us from the crowd and had announced that he was going to beat us up. I suppose the children thought it at least as good a show as the movie, as a large group had congregated to watch. The boy, a Hispanic kid a head taller than I, stood in front of us, taunting us with his fists and calling us chickens, while we stood against the cinder-block wall of the theater, outnumbered and frightened.

Finally, deciding a good beating would be less painful than the humiliation, I told the boy that I would fight him. Tucking my thumbs in my clenched fists I began weaving and bobbing, mimicking what I had seen boxers do on TV. Though fighting was part of the routine at home, we did not really punch. We wrestled and twisted and pinched and choked, but for all the torture doled out by the brothers, punching took something malicious that we did not possess.

Being defended by his little brother was too much for Van. Before a single punch was thrown, he pushed me aside, then commenced to beat the stuffing from the boy. Van did not stop, even when the bully, bloodied and crying on the ground, pleaded for mercy and then for his mother. I remember feeling a great deal of satisfaction as the children the bully had gathered to witness our demise now laughed at him.

When our mother arrived a few minutes later in our green, wood-paneled Chrysler station wagon, not one of us told her about the incident. I suppose we were protecting her. In all my years in California I had seen only one fight, and it was pretty much by mutual consent of its participants. I decided then that Utah was not civilized, and I suppose that that particular neighborhood still isn't.

Still, those days were not without joy. The old house stood at the end of a dead end street and had several acres of wooded land and a large creek that ran through it. It was ideal for a family of boys. We had BB-gun fights (though we younger siblings were mostly just used as targets for the older brothers, as we ran from tree to tree while they shot at us) and we navigated the creek that ran alongside the house, looking for gold. At one point the creek ran into a bramble thicket that we could not penetrate until we built a wood-plank raft that rested on top of tire inner tubes. Lewis and Clark could not have felt a greater thrill of adventure as we launched our craft upstream and floated to uncharted areas, wondering if we'd return alive. We did not find gold but we encountered some furry, muskratlike mammal, and that was just as good.

We caught grasshoppers and spiders, tried them for being ugly and executed them. We dropped ants into fields of ant lion pits, watching with fascination as the lions would suddenly emerge to drag their prey below. Once we had a water snake harvest and filled a gallon ice cream bucket with snakes, which, to my mother's horror, we forgot to tell her we had left in the pantry.

In addition to the four-bedroom house where we lived, there were numerous antiquated structures begging to be explored, for they were locked and had not been entered for years. These included a potato cellar, a chicken run, a toolshed filled with mysterious ancient rusted artifacts and an old green house with a thousand broken panes of glass. It was our duty, as boys, to seek out and destroy every pane that had somehow survived time.

And there were trees to be climbed. Willow, maple, sugar maple, weeping willow and tree of heaven. When we were hungry there were apple trees—Jonathan and red Delicious, plum trees and Bartlett pear and at least one black walnut. We would fill our pockets with walnuts, then carry them to the concrete sidewalk and break them open with hammers, prying the soft, white meat from the wrinkled shells. We would eat them until they gave us canker sores.

Though we climbed every tree big enough to hold us,

our favorite was the giant, thick-stumped box elder that towered above the irrigation ditch in the front of our yard. The tree was far too wide to climb without a ladder, so we gathered pieces of wood and rusted nails from the shed and pounded steps into the tree until we were able to scale its heights. The brothers had tied a rope to it, with a pulley fastened to bicycle handlebars, so that we could ride down it, screaming across the yard.

One quiet Saturday afternoon Van and I decided to climb the tree. It was just the two of us that day, as our older brothers had all gone to Bear Lake in northern Utah, to work with my father, who, in spite of his master's degree, had gone back to his earlier profession as a building contractor.

As Van climbed above me, a loud buzz suddenly split the air.

There are moments of our lives that are burned in the most precise detail into the flesh of our memory. This is one such moment for me. I was still clutching to our makeshift ladder when Van fell past me, his face inches from mine, his eyes bulging from their sockets like a cartoon caricature. He fell about sixteen feet to the dirt and root-laced ground below, landing with a loud thud. Seeing his lifeless body sprawled out below me, I shimmied down from the tree, then ran to the house, screaming all the way for my mother.

My mother emerged to see her child lying motionless

on the ground, his eyes closed, his skin black. With me crouching beside her, she knelt down and gently shook him as she called his name. To my relief, Van's eyes suddenly flitted, then slowly opened. He began to moan. "Is it true?" he asked. "Am I really dead?"

By nightfall, I learned what had happened to my brother. Van had started to slip and, reaching out for a branch, had grabbed instead on to a nine-thousand-volt power line that the tree had grown around.

I remember looking at my brother's hand. The electricity had burned through his flesh, leaving the power line's imprint deeply melted into his fingers, erasing his fingerprints, as it passed through his body and blew out the soles of his shoes.

The doctor told us that an electric shock of that magnitude would almost certainly kill someone—especially a child. He believed that my brother had been dead and that, fortuitously, the long fall to the ground had started his heart again, like CPR. This was purely conjecture on his part, for electricity is a peculiar thing and what might kill one person won't kill another. I am told that's why death row inmates are shocked three times in electric chairs. Still, the chance of surviving such a shock is pretty slim.

My grandfather came to see us the next day. After talking to Van for a while he examined his deeply burnt and blistered hand, then anointed my brother's head with a few drops of olive oil. Then he laid his own hands on my brother's head and blessed him, so that he would be healed without mark or scar. Several weeks later, when the doctor unwound the bandage, the hand was perfect. Even the fingerprints were back. "There's a force at work here I don't understand," the doctor said to my mother.

I don't think my mother was all that surprised.

2

◆

DESTINY

*Believe. Believe in your destiny and the star from which
it shines. Believe you have been sent from God as an
arrow pulled from his own bow.
It is the single universal trait which the great of this earth
have all shared, while the shadows are fraught with
ghosts who roam the winds with mournful
wails of regret on their lips.
Believe as if your life depended upon it.
For indeed it does.*

THE LOCKET

$\mathcal{A}$T SOME POINT EVERY one of my siblings received a blessing from my grandfather. They were not all healing blessings, as had been my brother's; rather they were similar to the kind written about in the Old Testament, as when Isaac blessed his son Jacob. Every blessing given to us was unique and spoke to us individually of the journey we would walk on this earth. Most of my grandfather's blessings were counsels on how to live righteously, though portions were prophetic of the challenges and opportunities that would come to us.

One afternoon, shortly after I had turned twelve, I went with my parents to my grandfather's house. After talking with me for a short while, my grandfather laid his hands on my head and began to speak. Among the many words of his blessing he told me that someday I would "walk with the royalty of this earth and be known as one who loves God."

As we left his house I asked my mother, "Does that mean I'm going to be famous?"

I sensed that my mother was not pleased with what I had taken from the blessing. "You must not talk of such things. What Grandpa told you was sacred."

The blessing had been recorded on my grandfather's old reel-to-reel tape recorder and was later transcribed by my grandmother and given to me. I pasted it inside the cover of one of my journals.

It was odd to me that I would be given such a promise, and though it had left me with a pervasive sense of destiny, it was, I suppose, without faith. I was too unlikely. I spent most of my childhood alone. Outside of my brothers, I had few close friends. I had chronic acne, severely cowlicked hair and nervous tics that amused or annoyed the other children at school. I struggled constantly with feelings of inadequacy. Such a destiny belonged to someone else. Someone, at least, with clear skin.

3

◆

C A FALL

*My teenage years were uneventful and significant
only to myself.*

THE CHRISTMAS BOX

*C*IRCUMSTANCES GRADUALLY improved for our family. My father had a run of work and we purchased a lot in a better part of Salt Lake. We worked together to build our home, from pouring the foundation to hanging wallpaper. Every room of our home was unique. My bed was in a tree, while my sister's hung from chains. Scott and Mark wallpapered their room with a Yamaha motorcycle billboard.

The future again looked promising. "The only way I'll leave this home is in a pine box," my mother was fond of saying. She didn't. As quickly as we had gotten back on our feet, my father was off his. My father fell through a staircase on a construction site and broke both of his legs, shattering one of his ankles in seven places. The doctors fastened his legs back together with pins and wrapped him in casts up to his hips. He was laid up in bed for nearly a year.

Unfortunately my father did not have insurance. Early in my parents' marriage they had purchased health insurance, only to be denied coverage when they finally made a claim. My father decided then that the entire insurance industry was a scam.

With neither medical nor disability insurance, circumstances again turned bad and again we put our house up for sale, moving to a small three-bedroom duplex a few miles east of the home we had built for ourselves.

> *Rich company, like rich food, is often a cause for indigestion. . . .*
>
> THE LOOKING GLASS

In some ways it was not so bad leaving the neighborhood. We had built our home near a country club, where most of our neighbors were rich or at least severely comfortable. And we weren't.

I'm not claiming poverty. I have walked the jungles of South America and backlands of Asia on humanitarian missions and seen true poverty. Even as a child I knew there were millions in America who had less. But in that neighborhood I learned class distinction in subtle yet unmistakably clear forms. I vividly recall sneaking into the country club while my friends walked in through the front gate because I did not have a dollar to be their guest. I remember not being allowed in one child's home because his mother did not like my clothes. I also remember with stinging clarity a friend telling me that his parents said he could not exchange Christmas gifts with me because I would not be able to buy something good enough.

◆

A few years ago Pulitzer Prize–winning journalist Rick Bragg and I were speaking at an exclusive club in the South, discussing our books with a crowd of mostly wealthy women. Rick was introducing his book *All Over but the Shoutin'*, his story of growing up poor in Alabama. As he spoke of the pain and discrimination of his impoverished youth—he'd been raised by a single-parent mother who picked cotton and took in the laundry of the other kids at school—I realized the thickness of the scars I still carried.

As we left the event, the woman who was driving me that day, a middle-aged woman born with a silver foot in her mouth, turned to me and said, "That boy just needs to get over it." We had a very quiet afternoon.

In that neighborhood I would sometimes seek to alleviate my feelings of inferiority by remembering the blessing my grandfather had given me. Someday I'll be somebody, I told myself. But it seemed so distant and so improbable.

◆

Our financial travails were especially hard on my mother, amplified by the care of eight children. Most of my memories of my mother at this time were of her in bed in a darkened bedroom. My friends thought she was going to die. At least they told me so.

My mother suffered from depression, complicated by severe PMS. Neither the medical profession nor society knew much about such things at that time. It was an era when Valium was handed out like aspirin to relieve middle America's housewives of their "anxiety," and those who suffered from depression were mostly just considered weak and sometimes sinful. It would be years before my mother received the help she needed and rightly deserved. In the meantime there was hell to pay.

One night I came home from a friend's house to find our foyer filled with people. One of my brothers' girlfriends took me aside.

"What happened?" I asked.

"Your mother slit her wrists. She's going to die."

Mom didn't die. But she didn't get better either. I remember we had an electric knife sharpener in the house. I couldn't tell you the name of my first-grade teacher, but I could draw a detailed picture of that knife sharpener. It was an avocado-colored can opener—blade sharpener in one, with a small doughnut-shaped magnet that held the can as you clamped down on it. It had a slightly sloped plastic appendage on its back with two small slits to run a knife blade through.

Several times, the first few weeks after that incident,

when I was home alone, my mother would go into the kitchen and sharpen a knife. The shriek of the grinding blade could be heard anywhere in the house. I remember hiding behind the couch and covering my ears while each pass of the knife sent shivers and sobs through my body. One night, after she had gone to bed, I stole the appliance. I wrapped it in towels and hid it beneath the downstairs bathroom sink.

◆

Mom is well now, active and blessing all of our lives. She happily tends to her raspberry bushes, and every July 24 she holds what she calls a "country fair" in her backyard, complete with homemade ice cream and lawn tractor rides, for her thirty-eight grandchildren. Three days a week she does volunteer work at the Christmas Box House for abused children.

I thank God for the advances in medicine that have freed her. I am also grateful to all those women and men who have had the courage to share their own stories of darkness. Especially my mother. She asked that I include this in my book as she believed it might help free someone else from their pain and give them hope that the sun will rise again.

I don't know what effect those experiences had on me. I like to think that I'm healed and that I learned patience and empathy. I like to believe that I'm a stronger man for it. But every now and then I feel those memories seep up through the lines of my writing like groundwater. And I realize that deep within me, there is still a little boy covering his ears and hiding behind the couch.

Dear Mr. Evans,

I saw your book for the first time at Christmas shopping for a very special gift for my mom. God has been working on my mom for years to reach her heart. In short, to remind her that she is special and is deserving of love. My mom has had a very hard life.

I was in a bookstore when I prayed to God to help me find the special gift I was looking for when, out of nowhere, I heard him say, "The Christmas Box." I had never heard of the book before. I looked at the cover but I did not pick up the book. I must have looked half the store over, but your book kept coming back to my thoughts. I believe it was God not giving up. So I went back, picked up the book and started reading. I am sure that the manager must have wondered about me. Before I knew it, I had spent a few hours in the store just reading your story. I realized this was my special gift to my mom. God was so right. It will show her what is most important of all, "Love."

Again, thank you so much and God bless you and your family.

Love in Christ,

Shantay

4

◆

THE
COLT
ROUNDUP

$\mathcal{E}$VEN THOUGH I OFTEN wrote for fun, my first serious thoughts of becoming a writer came as a sophomore in high school, when I decided to try out for a staff position on the high school newspaper, the *Colt Roundup*. I was turned down.

Not willing to give up, I came up with another plan. I had seen the *Roundup*'s editorial cartoons and even though I was not an artist, I believed I could do better. I went to the newspaper adviser and asked if they needed a cartoonist.

"Show me something," he said. That night I went home and drew a cartoon. It was a fairly recognizable likeness of President Jimmy Carter, with pins stuck in him, each labeled with one of the myriad crises that plagued his administration. Beneath it was the tag line *GOP Voodoo Doll*.

It wasn't *Doonesbury*, but the journalism teacher, Pete Sorenson, liked the cartoon enough that he introduced me to the staff as the new cartoonist. It was a great in, even if it was through the back door.

Although I had no aspirations to be a cartoonist, I

planned to just bide my time until opportunity reared its head. My break came sooner than I expected. By the third staff meeting one of the reporters failed to turn in his story. I offered to write it for him. I turned it in the next day, and to the editor's surprise, it was good enough to print. From then on I was given writing assignments in addition to my cartoons, which were gradually improving.

This was just the beginning. As the novelty of being on the newspaper staff wore thin, so did the staff. One by one the reporters dropped off, missing assignments or refusing them, sometimes both. Once our frustrated editor in chief ran a blank page with a note that read, "This space was supposed to be filled with a story by so-and-so, who did not think it important to meet his deadline."

By the end of the year I was the acting feature editor of the *Roundup*. I've heard it said that half the secret to success is just showing up. It may be true.

5

TUXMANIA

"And what is your situation in life?"
"I'm a recent college graduate with a degree in business.
We moved to Salt Lake City to start
a formal wear rental business."
"Such as dinner jackets and tuxedos?" she asked.
"That's right," I said.
She took mental note of this and nodded approvingly.

THE CHRISTMAS BOX

$\mathcal{I}$ ALWAYS HAD A JOB. They were usually temporary positions, something along the line of collecting shopping carts at the local Woolworth's for a nickel apiece or cleaning movie theaters. One summer I painted house numbers on curbs. My first real job with a time clock was at a Taco Time. I wore a paper cap and shoveled soybean-laced taco meat into taco shells passed along a rail. A few years later I moved up the pay scale, first as a dishwasher at Italian Village Restaurant, then again as a busboy at an upscale French restaurant called La Caille. Then, during my senior year of high school, a friend told me there was an opening at Tuxedo Junction, the formal-wear shop where he worked. The pay was low, but working with formal wear was a lot cooler than washing dishes or busing tables. And there were perks—free tuxedos for the proms. It was too good to pass up.

Two brothers, Gordon and Eldon Fletcher, owned the

business. They were good men, as were my coworkers, and Tuxedo Junction became my home away from home.

I graduated from high school, was voted by my class "the most likely to die saving hostages" (don't ask; I don't know) and enrolled at the University of Utah. I kept my job at Tuxedo Junction, though I changed my hours to reflect my new schedule, working weekends and evenings.

One Saturday I noticed Gordon Fletcher lowering a large box through a trapdoor in the floor. I asked him what he was doing.

"Getting rid of another line of suits," he said.

I learned that the basement was filled with worn and outdated tuxedos and their accessories—ruffled shirts, dickies and cummerbunds—which they planned to store until they got around to throwing them out. I asked if I could sell them instead. The Fletchers didn't know why anyone would buy them, but deciding that they needed to clear them out of the basement eventually, they told me that if we cleaned out the basement on our own time, we workers could keep half of what we brought in from selling the tuxedos.

I spent the rest of the day devising strategies for selling the used suits. I created my first advertising campaign. I called it *Tuxmania*. For a week I ran tiny teaser ads in the local *Pennysavers* and in the classifieds section of the University of Utah newspaper.

Q. What's bigger, Tuxmania or a
    James Watt protest rally?
A. The rally.

To the woman I met at the Union cafeteria last
Thursday. I'll meet you at Tuxmania.
—The Mannequin

A week later I spelled out the details of the sale.

Tuxmania, Utah's only used tuxedo sale.
Coats, pants, ruffled shirts and ties.
Tuxedo Junction. 3300 South 1200 East.

The store went nuts. We sold the old suits to high
school drama departments, costume companies, college
students, even the homeless.

The entire advertising campaign cost me less than forty
dollars, and in the end we brought in more than sixteen
thousand dollars in sales. It also made me a hero with my
coworkers, for we pocketed close to two thousand dollars
apiece, and I got a steak dinner from the owners. I paid off
my car, a '69 Ford Fairlane, and saved the rest.

6

TAIWAN

The noble causes of life have always seemed foolish to the uninspired. But this is of small concern. I worry less about the crucified than those who pounded the nails.

THE LETTER

$\mathcal{W}$HEN I TURNED NINE-
teen, I sold my car, and using all the dollars I had managed
to squirrel away, I volunteered to serve a mission for my
church.

I was sent to the city of Kao-hsiung, in southern Taiwan. My only previous contact with Taiwan was the *Made
in Taiwan* label that seemed to be attached to everything
that wasn't made in Japan.

Taiwan is a tobacco-leaf–shaped island, a lush, tropical
country about a hundred miles off the southeast coast of
China. Culturally it's a microcosm of mainland China and
is largely populated by the Chinese nationalists who fled
Chairman Mao and the Communist Party.

Educationally my time in Taiwan was a remarkable
experience. I learned to speak Mandarin well enough
that I once got in an argument with a Chinese woman
on the telephone who thought I was lying when I told
her I was an American. The food was good and the cli-

TAIWAN

mate, with the exception of a couple of typhoons, was tolerable.

The work was another matter. Teaching Jesus to Buddhists and Taoists was not a highly successful proposition. I should have gotten used to rejection, but I never did. It hurt just as much to have a door slammed in my face my last day in Taiwan as it did the first.

In many ways I grew up in those years. I learned that standing for what you believe in often meant standing alone. And in spite of my frequent bouts of homesickness, I learned that I was fortunate to have so much to miss so badly.

I did see a few lives changed, and maybe that's the best you can take with you. That, and the lessons. It was in Taiwan that I learned the very real power of prayer.

Once, my companion and I were riding our bicycles in the country outside Chang-hua, a city in central Taiwan, when a motorcycle gang took an interest in us. Actually they were a motor scooter gang; the hoodlums in Taiwan rode Vespas, not Harleys. They got off their scooters and began gathering rocks, then they revved their scooters and headed toward us, no doubt intent on stoning us. We were alone on the road and had no place to go. We both said silent prayers and rode our bikes ahead as if we were unconcerned. As one of the motor scooters neared me, less than three feet away, the man on back threw his rocks at my face point-blank. I heard the rocks hit my bike and all around me, but not one of them struck me. I looked back at the rider, who had a look of astonishment on his face. I saw him shake his head as they drove off.

On another occasion we were driving a new Ford van to a remote town on the east side of the island when the van broke down. We were probably fifty miles from the nearest mechanic and we hadn't even passed a car for more than a half hour. After opening the hood and looking around for something that didn't look right (which is something all men do even if they don't know a carburetor from a cantaloupe), we knelt and prayed.

Within ten minutes a car appeared in the distance. The car slowed as it neared us, then pulled over, and a man got out. He was a mechanic. Not just any mechanic, but a Ford mechanic. And he just happened to have his tools in his trunk. He fixed the van and, refusing payment, drove away.

No matter how skeptical you may be, the odds of that are past ridiculous. I would be intellectually dishonest to call that a coincidence and ungrateful to not credit providence.

7

◆

KERI
DISERA

*Upon graduation from high school, I enrolled in college to
learn the ways of business, and in the process learned the
ways of life; met, courted, and married a fully
matriculated, brown-eyed design student named Keri.*

THE CHRISTMAS BOX

$\mathcal{W}$HEN I RETURNED HOME from my mission, I went back to the University of Utah. Deciding that what the world really needed was another lawyer, I declared a communications major and immersed myself in school. Tuxedo Junction had no openings, so I applied at the University of Utah *Chronicle* as a part-time reporter and was hired. But after just a few stories, I decided that I didn't like working for the paper and quit.

In truth my greatest interest wasn't writing or school. It was Keri Disera. Just before leaving on my mission, my best friend had brought his girlfriend over to meet me. It wasn't love at first sight. I don't think either of us was very impressed. Keri was a varsity cheerleader, fresh faced and preppy, and I was a longhaired debater type whose wardrobe consisted mostly of surgeon blues or camouflage fatigues from the army-navy surplus.

My friend left that summer, six months before me, on a church mission. He asked me to take care of his girl. I did.

A little too well, I guess. Keri and I started hanging out every day and soon became best friends. In addition to my job at Tuxedo Junction I had a night job as a watchman at the entrance of some condominiums. Keri worked at an ice cream parlor called Snelgroves. A couple nights a week, after she got off work, she would bring caramel-banana malts and her guitar and sit on the floor of the guard shack while I waved cars on through. Once a car stopped. "Do you have a girl in there?" an old man asked.

"Yes, sir."

He gave me the thumbs-up and drove on.

Keri and I would play music, eat and talk about the meaning of life, her boyfriend and all the girls I was dating.

When summer ended and Keri left for school, I moped around for days in a stupor before I realized the truth: I was in love with my best friend's girl. When I called Keri that weekend, I knew it was mutual, as she could not conceal her excitement to hear from me. A few weeks later I asked her out on a date and she accepted. I suppose it was our coming out. Word quickly got back to my friend, but he didn't seem concerned. He knew I was planning on leaving on a church mission as well and he had six months to win her back before I returned.

He didn't. When I returned home, Keri was still unattached. We had written nearly every week while I was in Taiwan, and though we were both keeping our options open, we were hopeful that something might reignite. Three months after my return, Keri and I began talking about marriage.

Keri's father, Larry Disera, wasn't too keen on the idea. Actually, he wasn't too keen on me. Larry was a gruff Italian Catholic, short of stature, big of nose and tough as a miner. Before his retirement, he was a union negotiator for Kennecott Copper Mine. In retrospect I suppose his aversion to me was a blessing, as he became the model for Dr. Murrow, the stern father in *The Locket* and *The Carousel*.

When I told Keri that I thought it would be proper for me to ask her father for her hand in marriage, she emphatically replied, "No!"

"Why?"

She looked at me as if I was stupid. "He doesn't want me to marry you. He doesn't even like you."

The evening we announced we were engaged, her father growled, "You better take care of her. I didn't raise her for twenty-one years for you to keep her barefoot and pregnant."

8

◆

POLITICS

$\mathcal{I}$T WAS AT THIS JUNCTURE
that fate played the first of many hands. In keeping with
my promise to keep Keri well shod, I started looking for
full-time work along with my schooling. I had never had
trouble finding work, until then. I became less picky as the
weeks waned, until I started to apply for about everything
I saw. I was rejected for three different custodial jobs.

After several months of rejection, I interviewed with a
local bank for a teller position and was told by the bank
manager that I was perfect for the job. She said I would be
taking the place of an employee who was leaving, so I
would have to wait a few weeks until the position opened.
She gave me a number to call and the date I would start.

I called the bank a week later, only to be told that someone had transferred from another branch and taken the position. Dejected, I hung up the phone. Within seconds, it
rang. The woman on the other end of the phone was Bae
Gardner, assistant director of the University of Utah's

Hinckley Institute of Politics. She wanted to know if I was available to go to Washington, D.C.

Years before, I had turned my name in to the institute for a possible position as a political intern. Ms. Gardner had called to tell me that a U.S. senator from Utah had an opening for an intern in Washington. I thanked her for the call but told her I would have to decline, as I was about to get married and needed full-time employment at home. She said, "If you're interested in politics, I might have what you're looking for. The Norm Bangerter for Governor campaign is looking for someone to work full time."

"Who's Norm Bangerter?" I asked.

"Representative Bangerter is the speaker of the Utah House of Representatives. He's running for governor."

She gave me the campaign's phone number and I called for an interview. At the time, Bangerter was a long shot, running fifth in a field of five candidates. But it was a full-time job, if only a temporary one, and it paid eight hundred dollars a month. And I got it.

I fell in love with politics and put my whole heart into my job. The campaign manager, Doug Foxley, noticed my efforts, and as my candidate rose in the polls, I rose with him. Within months I was promoted to campaign field coordinator for Salt Lake County. I was responsible for recruiting Bangerter supporters to run as delegates for the state convention.

Bangerter won the party nomination, then the general election. My candidate was now in office and politics was in my blood. I was also introduced to a new profession. The most enviable guys in the campaign were the advertising consultants. They were witty, dressed cool, commanded the candidate's respect and, from what I could see, made gobs of money. All that for just coming up with an idea now and then. I decided that I wanted to be an adman someday.

The week after the campaign ended I sat down with the campaign manager, who was talking to everyone on the staff about future aspirations. "You did well," he said to me. "But you're still a kid. Go back to school."

I did.

9

◆

THE COLLEGIATE

Some people were born to work for others. Not in a mindless, servile way—rather they simply work better in a set regimen of daily tasks and functions. Others were born of the entrepreneurial spirit and enjoy the demands of self-determination and the roll of the dice. Much to my detriment, I was born of the latter spirit.

THE CHRISTMAS BOX

$\mathcal{K}$ERI AND I WERE MAR-
ried midway through the campaign. Now, with the campaign over, I was again unemployed. Instead of looking for a job, I decided to pursue a dream. One of my campaign duties entailed working with college newspapers. I decided to publish my own. I called it the *Collegiate*.

From my past newspaper experience I believed that every paper needed a cartoonist. Seeking better talent than myself, I approached a former cartoonist for the U of U *Chronicle* named Evan Twede. Evan was no longer a college student but now the co-owner of a successful new Salt Lake advertising agency. He agreed to provide two cartoons a month. He didn't need the pittance I offered him, he simply wanted the opportunity for creative expression.

At best the *Collegiate* was a hand-to-mouth existence. But I earned at least as much as I would waiting tables, and it provided me a unique educational experience as well. I learned to run a business, as well as manage a staff. I caught an employee embezzling from me and made him pay me back. And I learned firsthand the power of the press. When the university was about to shut down *Newsbreak,* a campus news broadcast program that had produced some of Utah's most successful television journalists, I ran a cover story on the proposed closure with a cartoon drawing of a television set with an ax raised above it. The headline read, "Will the Ax Fall." It saved the program.

Still, after a year of publishing the *Collegiate,* I decided I had had enough. I was just going to close down my paper when, on a whim, I decided to see if anyone would buy it. I ran a classified ad offering the paper for sale for seven thousand dollars—a number I had pulled out of a hat. I had two calls and sold the *Collegiate* within a week.

That same week I visited our cartoonist, Evan, to tell him that I would no longer require his services. He seemed much more interested in the amount I had made from selling my paper than in my decision to close it down. That weekend he called me at home to offer me a job. He and his business partner had just broken up the agency and he was looking for a business manager for his new firm, Evan Twede Advertising. I told him I would take the job if I could stay in school. He agreed.

As the agency grew, school grew painfully tedious. Moreover, what I learned in school about advertising seemed mostly outdated and largely irrelevant. I endured only two more quarters before I dropped out.

10

◆

JENNA

. . . not fifteen months from the ceremony, [Keri] gave birth to a seven pound, two ounce daughter whom we named Jenna.

THE CHRISTMAS BOX

$\mathcal{T}$HERE WAS ANOTHER MO-
tivation to my wanting to work full time. Keri had just quit her job to give birth to our first child: a beautiful daughter we named Jenna. I fell madly in love with this little girl. And fatherhood.

Ironically, early in our marriage I had no desire to have children—a postnuptial discovery that left Keri panicked. As odd as it seems now, we had never discussed children before getting married, I because I was not interested in them, and Keri because she had just assumed that anyone coming from such a large family would want them. It's not that I didn't like children. I just thought of them in the same way I thought of boats—occasionally fun, but not worth the trouble of ownership.

The not-so-subtle pressure to "breed" from parents and grandparents made me even more resistant to the idea. Keri and I eventually learned to limit our discussion of children because it always led to fights.

Then, one night at a party, I ran into a friend I hadn't

seen for a while. I had always considered him a worldly guy, and I was surprised to hear him spouting the virtues of fatherhood. Later that evening he cornered me. "You have no idea what you're missing," he said. "Having children is the greatest thing out there. Nothing in life has made me this happy." I gave him my well-rehearsed "Thanks but no thanks" speech, but that evening I began thinking about what he had said. Suddenly I felt a strange new feeling I would best describe as a curious strain of homesickness. I felt an intense longing *for a child.*

The next morning I told Keri I was ready. Keri was not only surprised, she was flustered. It was easy to push against a wall knowing it was immovable. "I don't know if *I'm* ready," she said. A week later she decided that she was. Ten months later Jenna was born.

11

◆

RICK EVANS IS A MADMAN

It would seem that my Andrea is growing so quickly, as if time were advancing at an unnatural pace. At times I wish it were within my power to reach forth my hand and stop the moment—but in this I err. To hold the note is to spoil the song.

TIMEPIECE

$\mathcal{I}$ LOVED ADVERTISING. From producing television commercials to designing direct mail campaigns, I got my hands in all of it—an advantage of working in a small agency. The California Raisins were the rage back then, and in my spare time I taught myself the art of clay animation and produced a clay animation television commercial, an animated couch potato named Otis Spud.

I had worked at Evan Twede Advertising for only two and a half years when the entrepreneurial bug bit me and I decided to leave to start my own agency. Evan and I parted amicably and I hung out my own shingle.

To advertise my new business I put up signs on the sides of city buses. The bus cards read, RICK EVANS IS A MADMAN. A few weeks later the message changed, and a big red X crossed out the M. The banner now read, RICK EVANS IS AN ADMAN, CALL FOR SOME SANE ADVERTISING ADVICE.

Things went well at first. I picked up a large client my first day in business, and three of my campaigns won local

Addy awards. My salary doubled the first few months. But success was short-lived. After six months one of my clients went out of business, leaving me with a stack of unpaid bills. At the same time my other clients cut back on their advertising budgets. To make matters worse, I contracted mononucleosis, and for nearly five weeks it was all I could do to not fall asleep at my desk. I worked constantly and worried always. As I overcame my illness I worked even harder trying to make up lost ground and keep my business afloat. Over the next year, I grew accustomed to working six days a week, coming home after dark every night.

Then came another change in our life. Keri gave birth to our second child, another beautiful girl. We liked two names equally well so we gave her both. We named her Allyson-Danica.

Though I saw nothing wrong with my new lifestyle, the truth was I was missing out on the better part of life; my little girls were growing up without their father. One evening all that changed.

There was nothing unusual about the evening. I had come home from work late, the lights were off in our apartment and everyone had already gone to bed. Allyson was asleep in her cradle in our bedroom while Jenna slept in her own room. Since I had not seen Jenna that day I decided to go in and check on her. As I opened the door to her room a distinct voice came to my mind. *You are trading diamonds for stones.*

I paused at the threshold, then I stepped inside the room. As I stood there looking at my child, the voice came again. *You have one childhood with your daughter. When it is gone, it is gone for all eternity.*

As the message sunk in I was suddenly filled with tremendous grief. I knelt at the side of Jenna's bed and wept. Then I picked up my sleeping daughter and held her. I made her a promise. I would be there for her. My destiny would have to wait.

Dear Mr. Evans,

I'm sure you receive many letters, and though this letter may never actually be seen by you, I felt compelled to write just the same.

At the risk of sounding melodramatic, I feel your book has touched my soul as to change my life. I oftentimes worry over my decision to quit work and stay home with my children. I thought perhaps I was doing them a disservice by denying them the advantages the extra money could provide. It was important that the character in your book, Mary Anne, was wealthy. The tragedy and sadness amongst all of their riches pointed glaringly to what would seem obvious but often is not. The really important things don't have price tags. I can now rest in my decision. The most important things I can give my children are not material things, rather the values that will carry them well through life. I must love them the best I can, leave the rest to God and hope for the best.

After reading your book I went into my daughter's room and watched her for a minute. As I was standing over her, she rustled to sleepy wakefulness. I bent down and wrapped my arms around her and held her close. She looked at me and asked, "Why are you crying?" How could she understand? How could I express all that I felt? I said, "I love you." She nestled into me and seemed content that it was enough.

I must go now. Inspired by your book, this is only the first of many letters I have to write. Thoughts long unspoken will be imparted in each letter. I don't want to someday regret what I didn't say.

Thank you sincerely,

Pamela

12

◆

ANOTHER
BLESSING

$\mathcal{O}$N THE BUSINESS FRONT, things did not improve. I learned that clients were far more dangerous than the competition. It seemed that every time I got ahead, one of my clients would sting me, leaving me with unpaid bills. After a few more years of struggling, I decided that I had had enough of advertising and its risks and decided to focus solely on clay animation. I moved my office to a warehouse and opened ClayMagic Productions.

Though we had a few successes, ClayMagic Productions never flew. All the while, I was steadily descending deeper into debt. Close to fifty thousand dollars' worth. I was receiving daily collection calls from nasty people, while my stomach acid digested my stomach lining. In spite of my promise to Jenna, I was now forced to work long days. In the final months of my business I was working up to a hundred and twenty hours a week just to stave off financial collapse.

All this time I did what I could to shield Keri and the

girls from our financial realities. I scrounged gas money and ate soup every day for lunch at a soup kitchen a few blocks from the warehouse where the bread sticks were free.

Finally I admitted defeat. I began closing down my business while I looked for a job, realizing that it would likely take a decade to pay off my business debts. Coincidentally, that same week I received a phone call from an old business associate I had not spoken with for more than a year. He said that he had recently heard of a job and for some reason kept thinking of me. It was a design and marketing position for a bank in Riyadh, Saudi Arabia. The pay wasn't great, but it was far more than I was making, and my salary would be tax free. Our family would have an adventure while I whittled away at my debts. It was, I decided, an answer to prayer. But when I prayed about the position, I felt a strong impression to stay put—that it was only a distraction. *A distraction from what?* I thought. Without knowing why, I turned down the job.

◆

Throughout this time I never forgot my grandfather's blessing. Now, as I was approaching the watermark year of thirty, my feelings of inadequacy ran unchecked. I was having a premidlife crisis. I was a college dropout, a failure at business and mired in debt. I was anything but famous. The promise of my grandfather's blessing could not have seemed more distant.

In retrospect, I suppose that I never doubted my grandfather's blessing, for my grandfather was, to me, infallible. I had witnessed too many miraculous things at his hands. What I really doubted was myself. I began to wonder if I had lived so much below my potential that I had betrayed the promise of my grandfather's blessing. This possibility weighed heavily on my mind. It was not the loss of fame and fortune that disturbed me, rather the fear that I had lost something much deeper and more costly. I wondered in my heart if I had let God down.

One May evening I was at my grandfather's house helping him with some chores, when I found my feelings particularly bothersome. At the end of the night I asked my grandfather if he had another blessing for me. He looked down for a moment, then said, "Yes. Come with me."

He led me to his den, laid his hands upon my head and, to my astonishment, he began to repeat, nearly word for word, the blessing he had given me twenty years previous—with one exception. He added a line. "My beloved grandson," he said with authority, "you are about to embark upon a mission that will touch the hearts of the children of men in a way you cannot now fathom."

I arrived home that night as confused as I had left. Nothing of that magnitude was happening in my life. I wrote my grandfather's words in my journal and promptly forgot them.

Then my former boss, Evan Twede, called. His agency was running a well-funded campaign for the Salt Lake City mayoral race, and having just broken up with his third partner, he asked for my help. He generously offered to split all the profits we made from the race. I accepted his offer.

Although we lost the race, our candidate had made it through the primary and come close enough to an upset that we made a name for ourselves. And for the first time in months, I had money. Enough, at least, to pay my bills at home.

It was at our candidate's "victory" party that we met a man who planned to run for the U.S. Senate. Robert F. Bennett was a tall, Lincolnesque man whose father had, years previous, been a U.S. senator from Utah. He was also a millionaire entrepreneur, one of the founding partners of Franklin Day Planners, a large Utah-based company.

As a young man, Bennett had gained some national notoriety as the man President Nixon had believed to be Deep Throat—Woodward and Bernstein's unnamed source who broke the Watergate scandal. In the Senate race Bennett was a long shot, but I liked Bennett and I wasn't in much of a position to be too picky with my clients. Besides, if you believe in the candidate, it's better business to take long shots. It's as a friend once told me: Always pick fights with people bigger than you. If you win, you're a hero. If you lose, you're courageous.

Bennett's candidacy came at the right time in my life. The Senate race turned out to be the most expensive Senate race in Utah history. In just six months I was able to pay off my business debt and still manage to put a little away.

And I was beginning to regain some of my lost confidence. In the heat of the campaign I decided to run for the state legislature.

13

◆

C A BOOK

*. . . creative causes must be dictated by passion, for
without passion we are doomed to mediocrity.*

THE LOCKET

$\mathcal{I}$T WAS PAST MIDNIGHT, election night 1992. Keri and I sat in a crimson-carpeted reception room of the Little America hotel, staring silently and red-eyed at a computer screen, awaiting the final vote count for my race. The hotel staff was tearing down the wet bar across from us. Somewhere the moan of a vacuum droned.

It was a presidential election year and the federal races had been decided hours earlier. Bennett had won in a landslide and William Jefferson Clinton had been declared America's forty-second president. Though there still came an occasional jubilant shout, they came with less frequency and voice. The crowds were gone, floating away with the television cameras. It was something I had noticed years before: the crowds always leave with the press. Now, at this hour, just a hatful of candidates, political groupies and lobbyists lingered, watching television and computer monitors as the election tallies of regional races came in from voting districts around the state. My race for the state legislature had been neck and neck all evening, sometimes within just a few dozen votes. When the final tally of my race flashed on the screen, neither of us knew what to say. Keri finally spoke. "You lost," she said softly.

I had lost by 1 percent, fewer than one hundred votes. As we walked out of the hotel, Keri took my hand. "Are you real upset?" she asked.

"I don't know. Ask me in the morning."

"I'm . . ." She paused for a moment, then confessed, "I'm just glad you don't have to be a legislator."

◆

It was as if fate had set me up for such a brief respite in my life. Bennett's victorious campaign had eased the financial burden of the previous years, and my own loss had left me with time on my hands. It was somewhere in this recess that I decided to do something I had never done before. I decided to write a book.

I don't recall the exact moment that I conceived the idea. If I had known the impact it would have on my life I probably would have recorded every detail surrounding it. But in truth, I considered it of such little importance to me that I did not even bother to write it in my journal or, for a while, tell anyone about it.

I had always heard that you should write from your own deepest experiences. I wanted to write something that

would express my love for my girls—something that cap-
tured the feelings of a father and the power of the love that
these little girls had brought into my life. I don't recall why
I decided to make it a Christmas story. I suppose it had
something to do with the fact that I planned to share the
book with my daughters around Christmastime. Or maybe
it was just because I love Christmas.

> *I love everything about this season. But I think what I love
> most about Christmas are its sounds. The bells of street
> corner Santa Clauses, the familiar Christmas records on the
> phonograph, the sweet, untuned voices of Christmas
> carolers. And the bustling downtown noises. The crisp
> crinkle of wrapping paper and department store sacks and
> the cheerful Christmas greetings of strangers. And then there
> are the Christmas stories.
> The wisdom of Dickens and all Christmas storytellers. . . .*
>
> THE CHRISTMAS BOX

As I began to write, the story came into my mind in tor-
rents of inspiration. I took to leaving notepads around the
house, as the words would come to me when I least expected: in the middle of the night, in the shower, early in
the morning. On one occasion I pulled off Interstate 15 to
write nearly an entire chapter, scribbling on the back of
envelopes and bills and whatever paper I could find in the
car at the time.

The story came to me like a jigsaw puzzle, with pieces here and there, while the final picture remained a mystery. For four weeks I wasn't sure what the book was about—until early one December morning, around 4 A.M., when the story woke me.

I climbed out of bed, retrieved a pen and paper and, in the predawn still, sat down at the kitchen table and began to write. Suddenly there came to mind something I had heard from a neighbor of mine, Leah Perry.

◆

Leah was an elderly woman and a widow of more than a decade. Initially my church had asked me to keep an eye on her. Our monthly visits were awkward at first, and even though she was lonely, I sensed that she didn't really want me around.

That changed one Christmas Eve. Keri and I were headed out to our traditional family parties when I remembered that I hadn't given Leah a gift I had bought for her. Keri was running behind, so I loaded Jenna and Allyson into the car and we agreed to meet at Keri's parents' house in an hour.

When we arrived at Leah's, the house was dark. Assuming that she was out, I left the gift on her doorstep; then, just to be sure, rang her doorbell. As I turned to go, I suddenly heard movement inside the house. Then the locks on the door slid and the door partially opened. Leah peered out. Her hair was uncombed and she wore a night-gown. I handed her the gift and she thanked me. As I turned to go, I was suddenly filled with sadness that she was alone on Christmas Eve. I turned back to her. "What are you doing tonight?" I asked.

"My kids are coming for me."

I nodded, said good night, and the door shut and locked behind me. Before we pulled out of the driveway the lights went back out. For a moment we sat in the car, then I turned to Jenna. "I don't think she's going anywhere, do you?"

Jenna shook her head.

I didn't feel right leaving her alone. I sighed, then the three of us climbed out of the car and knocked at her door. Again the locks slid and the door opened.

"If it's not too much of an inconvenience," I said, "my daughters have never seen a player piano. I thought maybe you could show them yours."

Her face lit up. I knew Leah well enough by then to know that the player piano was her pride. "Of course," she said.

We sat on her aged couch as Leah brought out roll after roll of music. She played every Christmas song she had, accompanied by our singing at the top of our lungs. After nearly an hour (and three times through "I Want a Hip-popotamus for Christmas"), I said, "Keri's going to be wondering where we are. We better go." We stopped at her doorstep. "I know your family's coming, but would you consider sharing Christmas Eve with us instead?"

She looked at me gratefully, but declined. "I better stay here," she said.

Our visits were never the same after that. I saw much more of her and she shared more of herself. I would sit back in her red couch, she in her La-Z-Boy lift chair from Sears (I remember the brand, as we had had at least two long discussions about her chair and its delivery), and she'd knit as we talked. We would usually talk about her kids or her deceased husband, Rod (Rod was a barber and a good dancer and she married him because he made her laugh), her health or her next operation. There was always an operation on the horizon. In the course of our visits Leah had both hip and knee replacements.

During one evening visit Leah was in a melancholy mood and began to reminisce. She told me that when she was little she lived up in the Avenues, next to the Salt Lake City Cemetery. Though it was forbidden, she and her sister would often play behind its walls. One day, while walking through the cemetery, she suddenly heard a horrible wailing. She looked up to see a woman kneeling at the base of a sandstone angel statue, clawing at the ground as if it held her from something she wanted desperately. After the woman left, Leah approached the statue. Etched in its stone base were three words: OUR LITTLE ANGEL.

◆

Now, nearly seventy years later, alone in our kitchen, I realized that the story of the woman at the angel fit perfectly in my book, bringing my entire story together, as if I had just placed a key piece of the puzzle. I understood, for the first time, that my story was about the pain my mother felt in losing a child.

At this moment something peculiar happened. I suddenly felt that I was not alone in the room. Moreover, I believed that I knew who was with me: my little sister, Sue, who had died when I was still a toddler.

Sue's death was not something our family spoke openly about. She was stillborn, and at the time, American culture did not openly acknowledge the hurt of such losses. My mother was sent home from the hospital with a rose and the consolation that she could always just have another baby. For months after her loss, friends and church members avoided her, unsure of what to say. My father, following the counsel of others, urged her to just get on with her life.

As a child I remember only a few instances of my mother speaking of Sue. Once, when I was around five, I found my mother alone in a room crying. Frightened, I asked her what was wrong.

"It's Sue's birthday," she said.

I believe that at that moment, at 4 A.M. in our small kitchen on Preston Street, Sue and I were reunited. I said out loud, "Sue, you gave me this story for Mom." As I spoke the words, it instantly came to my mind—in the same way the story had come to my mind—"Dedicate this book to me."

A few nights later, I presented the finished manuscript of my book to Keri, asking for her critique. I had not realized at the time that this was an intimidating thing to do to a wife: for either I had to be a good writer or she had to be a good liar. Initially, Keri tried to put it off, citing the late hour. I persisted. I asked her to read just the first few pages. If she didn't like it she didn't have to read it. "I'd understand," I lied.

Keri took the manuscript from me, went downstairs, sat on the couch and began to read. I took the pages from her as she read them. I soon noticed that she was actually engrossed in the book. An hour and a half later there were tears running down her cheeks. She finished my manuscript, set it aside and, for a moment, said nothing. I was brimming with anticipation.

"What did you think?" I asked.

She looked at me thoughtfully, then asked, "Where did you get that story?"

It was then that I told her about the experience I had had in the kitchen several days earlier.

"It makes me want to be a better mother," she said.

◆

Though I still had no intention of publishing my book, I felt compelled to share it with my mother and my siblings, as well as my daughters. I decided that I would make copies and give it out to my family for Christmas.

I set about making my book. I designed its cover, then typeset the book on my office computer. I then took my creation to a local copy shop and had twenty or so copies printed. On Christmas Eve I presented the copies to my family.

My mother was of Scandinavian descent, and growing up, we often followed Norwegian tradition, celebrating Christmas on Christmas Eve. As adults, my siblings and I still gather at my parents' house every Christmas Eve for dinner and a program. The routine is pretty much the same each year. Each family gives a presentation, a Christmas reading or skit—something to evoke the true spirit of Christmas—then Santa shows up in the den while a few adults stealthily pile the wrapped gifts hidden in the laundry room around the tree.

This year our family presentation was my book. My brothers were surprised to learn I had written something. I told them about my story, then presented a copy to each of my siblings. Though I sensed they were doubtful of its literary value, I felt wildly successful. I had intended to publish only two copies of my book, one for each of my daughters, and now I had twenty copies in print. I was done. At least I thought I was. The book had other plans.

14

◆

CHRISTMAS DAY

"Tell us, Richard, which of the senses do you think are most affected by Christmas."
I looked over at Keri. "The taste buds," I said.
Keri rolled her eyes.
"No. I take it back. I would say the sense of smell. The smells of Christmas. Not just the food, but everything. I remember once, in grade school, we made Christmas ornaments by poking whole cloves into an orange. I remember how wonderful it smelled for the entire season. And then there's the smell of perfumed candles, and hot wassail or creamy cocoa on a cold day. And the pungent smell of wet leather boots after my brothers and I had gone sledding.
The smells of Christmas are the smells of childhood."
My words trailed off into silence as we all seemed to be caught in the sweet glaze of Christmastime memories and Mary nodded slowly as if I had said something wise.

THE CHRISTMAS BOX

$\mathcal{C}$HRISTMAS AFTERNOON WE were lounging around my in-laws' house after dinner when I noticed my father-in-law (who had since decided that I was okay) pick up a copy of my book to examine it. I suspected he would soon put it down. He didn't. A few hours later I walked into the kitchen to find Keri and her sister laughing. "Ask Dad what he thinks of your book," Keri said.

"Why?"

"He came in crying."

Just then Larry walked back in. I suspect he had overheard his daughters, as he eyed us all grimly.

"What did you think of my book?" I asked.

"Don't push it," he said sternly. Then, as he walked away, he said, "It's a damn good book."

That evening, back at home, I received a phone call from one of my brothers. Given my family history, I fully expected a comment along the lines of "Rick, you have very poor punctuation." Instead he said softly, "Your little book has changed my life." The next day I received a similar phone call. And the next day. And the next. Every day that week someone called to share with me feelings about the book.

One of those calls was more important than I realized at the time. Three houses down from ours lived a friend of mine named John Stringham. John was an intellectual property attorney. I had given him a copy of the book, as I had several other neighbors.

John had accepted my book graciously (the same way one might accept a tuna casserole from a neighbor) but, he later confessed, doubted its merit.

One evening, out of curiosity, he began to read it. He finished it an hour later, in tears. He told his wife that she too needed to read the book. A few days later she woke him at two-thirty in the morning. She was crying hysterically.

"Is it true?" she asked.

He had no idea what she was talking about.

"That Christmas book. Is it true?"

The next day John came by the house. He said that he had noticed the copyright notice on the book but asked if I had taken the time to register it.

"No. It's just for my daughters."

"I think you better register this. I'll tell you what. I'll do it for you for free. There's a twenty-dollar federal fee that you can pay, but if not, I'll pay it myself."

◆

A few days later I received another phone call about the book. "You don't know me," the woman started, "but I've just finished reading your book and I thought it was wonderful. I just wanted to tell you how much your story meant to me."

"Thank you," I said. "Where did you get a copy of my book?"

"A friend of mine lent it to me." She told me her friend's name, which I also did not recognize. I realized that my book had been passed beyond my circle of family and friends. Out of curiosity I took a notepad and called all those I had given copies to and asked them with whom they had shared the book. Then I called them, and so on. I learned that in the four weeks since Christmas, those twenty copies had been read more than a hundred and sixty times.

Dear Richard,

I was deeply moved by your book, The Christmas Box. *It is a beautiful story and I cried while reading it.* The Christmas Box *was a connection to my recent tragedy only a mere three months ago, right before Christmas.*

On December 16, 1994, I labored and delivered a beautiful baby girl whom we named Belle. She was a stillborn. This experience has been and continues to be one of the most painful, intense, and lonely experiences I have ever gone through. In my incredible shock, pain, and grief I somehow survived the Christmas holidays with my children, my husband, and his family. Hearing certain Christmas carols brought me to tears. The pain was overwhelming. Your book helped me with one of my biggest fears. I wondered, will I ever enjoy Christmas again? I will always miss Belle, and Christmas will always remind me of her but I will see joy in Christmas again. Your message helped me to see that. Thank you.

About four days after Belle's birth, I had a very profound dream. A beautiful angel with a flowing white gown came into my bedroom and reached over me. She picked up baby Belle and then floated out of the room with her. She was very reassuring. The dream was very real and felt very right.

I look forward to visiting the Angel Monument in Salt Lake City and laying a white flower at its base. Thank you for sharing your story, The Christmas Box.

Sincerely,

Bege Reynolds

15

◆

REJECTION

I have learned a great truth of life. We do not succeed in spite of our challenges and difficulties, but rather, precisely because of them.

THE LOOKING GLASS

$\mathcal{M}$ORE THAN A MONTH after Christmas, I received a phone call from a local bookstore. The clerk at the store had been going through the Salt Lake City white pages calling all the Richard Evanses. There are more than a dozen such entries in the Salt Lake phone book and by the time she got to me, she had already called half of them.

"Hello, Mr. Evans?"

"Yes."

"Did you write a Christmas book?"

"Yes . . ."

"*The Christmas Box?*"

"Yes," I again replied.

There was an audible sigh of relief. "Oh, good."

"Who is this?"

She said she was calling from a local bookstore. "We'd like to know where we can order your book," she said.

"You can't order it. It's never been published."

There was momentary silence, then she said, "But we've

had ten orders for your book this week. Ten orders is pretty good for any book," she continued, "but for a Christmas book in February, well, that's unheard of. Maybe you should get your book published."

As I hung up the phone, I considered her suggestion. *Why not?* I thought.

◆

All I knew about getting a book published was that it's nearly impossible. In the next few days I sent my few remaining copies of the book to local publishers. They wasted little time in returning them along with a rejection letter. Thanks but no thanks. A book like this would never sell.

Still, the phone calls continued from people wanting to talk about how "the book," as it became known in our family, had affected them and asking where they could get copies of their own. By the time I received the last publisher's rejection letter, I had already decided that I would publish my book myself—as soon as I figured out how to do it.

Around this time I had a peculiar experience. I was at the public library when, out of curiosity, I typed *The Christmas Box* into the library's computer. Three different selections emerged. The title was already taken.

Disappointed, I began working on other titles for my

book but always came back to *The Christmas Box*. A few days later we had some friends over and were playing the game Trivial Pursuit when the question was asked of me, "Can the title of a book be copyrighted?"

Peculiar timing, I thought. "Of course it can," I replied.

"No, it cannot."

I kept the title.

◆

The first run of my book took nearly all of our savings. Eight thousand copies. I wasn't really sure how many books I should print. The fact that I chose to print eight thousand copies illustrates my complete naïveté regarding the publishing world. I chose eight thousand because I could think of eight bookstores that I thought would carry my book and I guessed that the average book title probably sold a thousand copies per store. I would later learn that the actual figure is closer to two and a half.

The first printing came off the press in late September of 1993. Those copies do not read "First Printing" anywhere on them for the simple reason that I never considered that there might be a second.

◆

There is something exhilarating about seeing your book in print for the first time. I suppose it's like witnessing the birth of a child, with all the joy of creation and the inherent wonder of the future.

With a book in hand I began making calls to bookstores. It did not go well. The bookstores did not share my enthusiasm. I learned that the retail book business does not take self-published books seriously. "Vanity publishing," they call it, conclusive indication of a book's lack of merit. In addition, it was simply too much of a bother for most bookstores to open an account for a publisher with only one book.

I was stuck with a mountain of books sitting in my printer's warehouse. I believe that my printer felt sorry for me after taking all of my money (and wanted my books out of the warehouse) and so she gave me a list of book distributors in the West. I called a small distributorship in Salt Lake City called Publishers Distribution Center. The president of the company, Bill Beutler, happened to answer the phone. I introduced myself, told him that I had recently written a book and was now looking for a distributor. I asked if he would be interested.

"We reject about ninety percent of what the publishers bring to us," he said. "Who's your publisher?"

I reluctantly admitted that I was self-published, but then told him about how the book was being passed on and about the call from the bookstore. He agreed to read it and I delivered it to him that very afternoon. I called back the following Monday and asked if he had had a chance to look at my book.

"I read it," he said.

"What did you think?"

He was slightly hesitant and I braced for bad news. "I hate to admit it," he said, "being a man, but it made me cry. Then my wife read it and she cried. She wants to give it to all of her friends this Christmas. We'd like to distribute your book. We think that you're going to do well with it."

I was elated. "How many copies do you think we'll sell?" I asked.

"We might sell as many as three thousand copies."

My heart sank. "Three thousand. Is that good?"

"Three thousand is *very* good. That's what the popular local authors sell over a holiday season, and no one knows who you are."

As I hung up the phone I thought, *I'll have Christmas presents for the rest of my life.*

16

◆

A
BOOKSTORE

$\mathcal{A}$BOUT TWO MONTHS after the release of my book, I was browsing in a Barnes & Noble bookstore when the store manager walked by. I stopped him.

"Excuse me. You sell my book here," I said. "I was wondering if you could tell me how it's doing?"

The busy manager looked at me with a dull expression. "What did you write?"

"It's called *The Christmas Box.*"

His eyes widened. "That's your book? It's actually doing very well."

"How many have you sold?"

"At least seven hundred."

"Is that good?"

He smiled at my question. "Yeah, that's good. That's as good as a new Grisham paperback release."

I was still too naïve about the industry to be impressed. "Yeah, but that's just a thriller. How's it doing compared to the rest of your Christmas books?"

"Christmas books? We've sold three times more copies of your book than the rest of our Christmas titles combined."

I smiled. "Pretty good."

"Pretty good," he repeated.

17

◆

THE
SNOWBALL
BEGINS

$\mathcal{T}$HE SECOND WEEK OF November, I received a phone call from Scott Beutler, the general manager of Publishers Distribution.

"I just wanted to tell you that we've already sold more than three thousand copies of your book and orders are increasing. You may have to print more books."

"How many should I print?" I asked.

Scott wasn't sure how to answer. After a moment he said, "Well, there's really no way of knowing."

I did the math. The warehouse still had five thousand copies and there were about six weeks left until Christmas. In order to sell out of my book we would have to sell almost twice the amount, in half the time. I didn't think it likely. And I was pretty much out of money. It seemed to me that if I printed a couple thousand more copies I would make enough to cover my debts and would still have books left over for the next season.

After struggling with what to do for several days, I decided to pray about it. As I prayed I had a very strong feeling to print twenty thousand more copies.

Bad inspiration, I thought. No one in Salt Lake City sells twenty-eight thousand copies of a book in twelve weeks. Not even John Grisham. Common sense told me that two thousand copies would be enough. But the message had been clear. I had even recorded it in my journal. In the end, I compromised between inspiration and common sense and settled on ten thousand more copies.

On December 9 my distributor shipped out the last of my first printing. The next day the new printing of ten thousand books was complete. Three days later I received another phone call from my distributor.

"We were wondering where the rest of your books are," Scott asked.

"What do you mean, 'the rest of my books'? The printer said that they had shipped all ten thousand to your warehouse."

"You only did ten thousand, then," he said, his voice laced with disappointment.

"Only?"

"Well, we've already sold them."

Ten thousand copies in three days. They were now shipping more copies *every* day than they thought I would sell in a year. I called the printer for more books and was told it would be impossible to have them printed before Christmas. I wished I had followed the inspiration I had received.

18

◆

THROWING
GASOLINE
ON THE
FIRE

$\mathcal{E}$VEN THOUGH THE BOOK-
stores' supplies of my books were diminishing, word of the book was still growing. Local bookstores began to complain to my distributor about the avalanche of phone calls they were getting for a book they couldn't get. Some said their phone lines were being jammed with calls, and asked us to do something about it.

What are we supposed to do? I thought. Then I had an idea. I had already paid for some radio commercials, which were now of no use to me. I wrote a new radio commercial that thanked all those who had purchased my book and told people that the book was sold out.

From this I learned a powerful marketing lesson: if you really want to sell a book, tell people they can't have it. It was like throwing gasoline on a fire. One bookstore manager told me that a fistfight had broken out between two women over the last copy of *The Christmas Box* in his store.

By Christmas day every copy I had printed was sold. I

had even depleted most of my own private stash of first editions, giving them to my advertising clients, with whom I would be back in business as soon as this author thing was over.

The Christmas Box had sold everywhere I had put it. And I had put it everywhere. Pharmacies, copy shops, doctors' offices, even hair salons. My hairstylist, as a favor to me, had started selling my book from her counter to her other clients. She said that she was making almost as much selling my book as she was doing hair.

One independent bookstore called to tell us that they had the last remaining stash of my books in the Salt Lake valley (they had forgotten to bring them out of their back room) and had doubled the price of my book and limited purchases to two per person. They had a long line outside their store until the books were gone. Years later another bookseller told me that *The Christmas Box* had saved her bookstore from bankruptcy.

I was receiving calls about my book every day. One of them was from Keri's friend.

She was getting her hair cut, she told Keri, when her stylist began talking about her father. She said that he had called her and asked if she would come see him. It was a strange request because she hadn't seen him for years. He was a difficult man and all his children had pretty much cut off contact with him. Then she called her brother and sister to see if he had called them as well. He had. None of them could figure out what he was up to. Finally they speculated that he must be dying.

A few days later, when they had all assembled at his house, he said humbly, "I've asked you here to see if you could ever forgive me for the father I haven't been to you. And if you could somehow allow me a second chance."

The children were stunned. After a tearful reunion one of the children asked him what had happened to bring about such a change. He told them that a few days earlier some people in the neighborhood had brought him a Christmas gift, a little book. He knew the people were religious and thought the book probably was as well, so he had no desire to read it. He put it aside. But he could not stop thinking about it. It bothered him so much that he threw the book away. But still it wouldn't leave his mind. In fact it got worse. It was as if the book was calling him. Finally he couldn't stand it any longer. Late at night he retrieved the book and read it cover to cover. Somehow it healed him. The strange thing, she said, is that it was just some little Christmas book called *The Christmas Box*.

◆

A few days after Christmas I received a call from a woman I didn't know.

"Are you the author of *The Christmas Box?*" she asked.

"Yes."

"I wanted to know if I could reprint a portion of your book. Our grandson died over the holidays and we would like to use a paragraph from your book on his funeral program. We found your book very comforting."

"Of course," I said.

These calls were the first trickle from the river to come.

Dear Mr. Evans,

As a producer of stage productions for Kansai Telecasting Corporation in Japan, I lead a very busy life. Awaiting the birth of my first son, I was not totally sure of how I felt about becoming a father.

My first son was born on January 1, 1994. This was also the same day I became aware of the book, The Christmas Box. Upon reading the book I was deeply moved by the message in it. I could not hold back the tears that rolled down my cheeks.

From then, your book became my Bible as far as being a father. Still now, I am not the perfect father but your story within The Christmas Box has greatly helped me in becoming a better father. I have intentionally kept my wife from reading this book for the express reason that I want her to think my changing into a more loving father has come from within myself, not from you and your book.

I hope that more people in Japan can read and feel the message I have come to know and love.

Akihito Kimura
Kansai Telecasting Corporation
Osaka, Japan

19

A LEAP
OF FAITH

*It is oftentimes a blessing to not know our limitations.
It's the only way to accomplish the impossible.*

RICHARD PAUL EVANS

I REALIZED THAT IF I COULD repeat the Salt Lake phenomenon on a national scale, my book would be the number-one-selling book in America. Maybe even the world. Again, my naïveté was a blessing. I did not understand how the national publishing machine operated—the power of chains, distributors and publishers and the deals that are made at New York publishing lunches. Salt Lake City was still sufficiently provincial that a small book could make it on its own merit. But competing with the "big boys," the large publishers and authors, was an entirely different matter.

Fortunately I didn't know this. The challenges I recognized already seemed insurmountable. Especially the marketing. My entire advertising budget was a meager seven thousand dollars. Senator Bob Bennett had just spent nearly 2 million dollars to sell himself just in Utah. Telling the entire country about my book with only a few thousand dollars of advertising would be like feeding thousands with one loaf of bread.

Of course, national media—a *Today* show or an *Oprah* appearance—would change everything, but the odds of being struck by lightning are greater than the odds of being on either show. Not having a publisher reduced my chances still more. Not even the local television stations were interested in my book. Being self-published, I learned, is like competing in the Olympics without a country—they make you run outside the stadium.

The hard truth was, I was an unknown with a little Christmas book. *If* this war could be won, it would have to be won in the trenches. I would have to visit as many bookstores and book trade shows as I physically could, hoping that word of mouth would quickly spread. It was like shooting flaming arrows into a dry field and hoping that a brushfire might start that would sweep the nation.

My biggest challenge was time. There's not much interest in Christmas books before Thanksgiving, and none after Christmas. That gave me a window of about five weeks to sell—not enough time for word of mouth to spread nationally. I needed to find a way to get the word out faster.

As I was contemplating this challenge, an idea came to me. I could give my books to radio stations as Christmas giveaways. I would give twenty-five books to each station, with the only requirement being that they give my book to listeners, with the tag line "If you read only one book this Christmas, it must be this one." The idea had possibilities, if the stations would do it. They likely wouldn't. No station wants to give away free airtime.

Still, I reasoned, there are more than seven thousand radio stations in the United States. I figured if I could get just a couple dozen of those stations to participate, it would be worth the attempt. I printed a postcard with the details of the offer and sent it out to every radio station in the country.

More than four hundred stations called back.

◆

The book tour I created for myself included several book industry trade shows. It was my best chance to meet booksellers from across the nation. The first show was the ABA's (American Booksellers Association) in Los Angeles, the mother of all book shows. I had no illusions. I was a small fish in a big pond. (Actually, a minnow in the ocean is a better metaphor.) Still, it was my best chance to get my book into booksellers' hands.

Publishers Distribution Center and I shipped three thousand books to the event, which we stacked in a large wall of books. With the help of Mike Hurst, the distributor's new sales manager, and the Beutlers, I worked the booth, handing free copies of my book to everyone who walked by. When not enough booksellers were coming by our booth, Keri and one of the other wives walked the floor of the conference hall handing out flyers until they were stopped by a security guard.

The show was memorable for several reasons. The first was meeting former first lady Barbara Bush. Mrs. Bush had come to promote her new book, *Barbara Bush: A Memoir.* I stood in line for about a half hour to meet her. I spoke with her for only a moment, just long enough to hand her a copy of my book, and was whisked away. (Years later she would invite me to speak at her literacy conference in Houston and I would spend several wonderful hours with her.)

That same day Mike pointed out a silver-haired man walking toward our booth. "That's Jack Canfield."

"Who's Jack Canfield?" I asked.

"He wrote a book that booksellers are predicting is going to be a big bestseller. It's called *Chicken Soup for the Soul.*"

Just then Jack walked up to me, followed by several others, who seemed to be in awe of the rising new author. Jack stopped and examined my stack of books. "May I have a copy?"

"Certainly." I handed him a book.

"Will you sign it?"

"You want my autograph?" I asked.

"Yes."

I took the book, signed it and handed it back to him. "Thank you," he said. Then, to my surprise, he leaned forward and hugged me. "Good luck," he said.

The greatest shackles we bear in this life are those forged by our own fears.

THE LOOKING GLASS

A few months later I attended the Mountains and Plains Booksellers Association show in Denver, Colorado. At first things weren't going quite as well as I had hoped. Even though there were a large number of booksellers in attendance, relatively few of them were in the exhibit hall, where we had rented a booth. Upon further investigation I learned why. The booksellers were either attending breakout sessions or were congregated in the outer hall where the author tables were set up.

It was a routine I would eventually become all too familiar with. Authors, sponsored by major publishers, came four or five at a time, flanked by their media escorts and book show personnel. They sat together at a long table and signed their books while booksellers by the score waited in line to receive not just free books but free *autographed* books.

Frustrated with the lack of interest in our booth, I had grabbed a stack of my books with the thought of handing them out to booksellers, but I lost my nerve when I saw the line. For several minutes I stood outside the velvet-roped stanchions enviously watching the authors greet the eager bookstore owners and workers.

Then I noticed a vacant chair between two of the authors. *Why not just sit down?* I thought. The idea was quickly extinguished by fear. Then, as I turned to walk away, I thought, How much do you care about this book? If you're not willing to fight for it, who will?

I turned back and walked to the side of the authors' table, then slid behind it. With a cursory nod to the authors at either side, I laid my books on the table in front of me and took a seat. To my horror, a member of the book show staff began walking toward me. Before she could speak, I looked up at her and said, "Sorry I'm late."

A subtle smile crossed her lips. "May I get you some water?" she asked.

◆

I returned to the same show the next year as an invited guest, and now the bestselling author at the table. The same woman was there from the year before. I said to her, "Do you remember me from last year?"

She nodded, with a wry smile.

"Thank you for not throwing me out."

"I almost did," she said, "then I thought, What's it going to hurt?" Then she added, "May I get you some water?"

20

◆

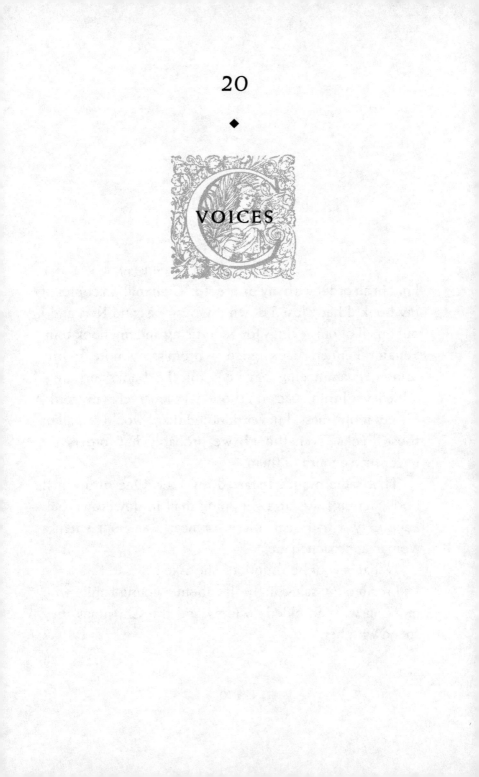

VOICES

$\mathcal{W}$HEN SEPTEMBER CAME I put in an order with my printer for a half million copies of my book. I had closed down my business, and Keri and I put up all of our savings for advertising and my book tour. Senator Bennett had signed a promissory note to the printer, guaranteeing payment for the books' printing. Whenever I think back on those days I marvel at my faith. Or my foolishness. I never doubted that I would sell all of those books, even though we probably had orders for fewer than a tenth of them.

That same month I started my tour. One of my first book signings was at a shopping mall in downtown Salt Lake City. I had been there for nearly an hour when a woman approached me.

"What is your book about?" she asked.

I recited my sales pitch. "It's about a young family who move in with an elderly widow and the Christmas they spend with her."

She looked disappointed with my reply. Then, to my surprise, she said, "I guess I need six copies. One for each child." Suddenly tears began to well up in her eyes as she corrected herself. "No, I'm sorry. I only need five copies. I've just lost a child." Then, in the crowded mall corridor, the woman began to cry. She was clearly embarrassed and when she had regained her composure she apologized. "I'm sorry. I don't know why I told you that. I don't even know why I'm standing here."

"I think I do," I said. "I've been told that this book is healing for those who have lost children."

She looked at me with a curious expression, then said, "Just a moment." She went into the store, purchased her copies, then brought them back out for me to sign. As I signed her books she suddenly asked, "Can you tell me what's happening to me?"

I looked up. "What do you mean?"

"I had already finished my shopping and as I was going back to my car I heard a voice. It said *'Go back inside, there's a young man waiting for you.'* When I came back inside I saw you sitting here and the same voice said, *'That's him. What he has, you need.'* "

She looked at me anxiously. "I can't believe this," she said. "I'm standing here crying and telling you that I'm hearing voices. You probably think I'm crazy."

"No," I said. "I don't."

◆

Three weeks later I was in Scottsdale, Arizona, signing books in Fashion Square Mall. At least, that was the plan. I had been in the bookstore for nearly forty-five minutes and the only attention I had received was from a woman who asked me to move so she could get to some books behind me. Suddenly a woman walked by my table and lifted one of my books, checked the price, then said, "I'll take one of these."

Mercy buy, I thought.

Her husband glanced at the book, then said disparagingly, "Man, you'll buy anything."

She bought the book and they left the store.

About twenty minutes later the couple returned. The man approached me, holding my book out in front of him. "I need ten more copies," he said.

"You've changed your mind?"

He leaned forward, his eyebrows bent. "There's something really weird about your book," he said in a hushed tone. "There's something mystical about it."

His wife came around to the other side of my table. "Do you believe in spiritual things?" she asked. "Like voices and promptings?"

"Yes," I said. "That's how the book came to me."

She glanced over at her husband. "We were in different

parts of the house tonight when we both heard a voice that told us to come here and find you. I don't know what this little Christmas book of yours is about, but whatever it is, we're supposed to share it."

21

◆

MAKING ANGELS

There is nothing so healing to oneself as to heal another.

THE LETTER

I WAS BACK IN UTAH, AT a book signing in a northern Utah shopping mall, when I noticed a woman across the mall staring at me. After a few moments she approached, hovering near my table as if afraid to speak to me. I spoke first.

"Would you like a book?"

She shook her head. "I've already read your book." Then she added, "You're not old enough."

"To be a writer?" I asked.

"To have experienced this story. The story isn't true."

"No, ma'am. It's mostly fiction."

"I wanted it to be true," she said softly. "I wanted a place to go. I wanted to lay a flower at the angel." Then she walked away.

The depth of the woman's sadness had a powerful impact on me. For the next few days the memory of her haunted me. I shared the experience with one of the salespeople at my book distributor.

"We get calls like that all the time," he said. "People are

always trying to find the angel. They wander through the Salt Lake City Cemetery looking for it. A lot of them say they've lost a child."

◆

I called Leah Perry, the elderly woman who had told me about the angel, and asked if she would take me to see it. We drove up to the southwest end of the cemetery and began combing the area she had run through nearly seventy years before. This was not easy for her, as she now hobbled along with a cane. We couldn't find the angel. After searching for nearly an hour, Leah raised her hands in frustration. Then, hitting a granite headstone with her wooden cane, she exclaimed, "It was right here by Mr. Bean!"

Leah called me the next day. "I phoned the cemetery," she said. "They said there was flooding in that part of the cemetery and some of the headstones were lost."

The angel was gone. As I thought of the grieving parents wandering the cemetery looking for it, I suddenly had the desire to rebuild the angel—to provide a place for them to grieve their little ones. When I told my mother of my desire, she began to cry.

"Sue was never buried," she said. "I have no place to go."

◆

Dear Mr. Evans,

I have just completed your book. Thank you so much for writing it. I bought your book in December but I got carried away with the bustle of the holidays and didn't get a chance to read it.

I didn't know it at the time but I was pregnant. We found out in early January. My husband and I were so excited. We felt so blessed. Our whole lives immediately revolved around this baby coming.

At fourteen weeks I had a miscarriage. It was the saddest and worst experience of our lives. The moment at the ultrasound when they said there was no heartbeat we were devastated.

Since there was no tangible way to mourn our loss—no grave to go to, no ceremony to take place—peace is hard to find. I felt left without resolution and just a lot of questions.

Your book has brought me some solace. I just want to thank you. Thank God I bought your book. I find it strange that I had it for so long and didn't read it. I guess it was waiting for me. I did send flowers to the Christmas Box Angel. That has also given me a sense of peace. Thank you for that and for helping me to heal.

Truly,

Karyn

I decided to have the angel in place before Christmas, less than three months away. I asked a neighbor of mine, a funeral director named Rob Larkin, if he knew where I could find an angel sculpture. I figured that morticians must have catalogues of premade statuary. Instead Rob asked me if I knew of a sculptor named Ortho Fairbanks.

"I don't think I could afford an original sculpture."

"You could never afford Ortho," Rob said, "but his son, Jared, is also a sculptor. He might be willing to do something."

I phoned Jared and told him my idea. He was interested, but insisted that I call his father.

"I can't afford your father," I said.

"You need to talk to him," he repeated.

The next day I met with Ortho Fairbanks and his wife, Myrna, in the front room of their home. The Fairbankses did not live far from me and I soon realized that I had met Ortho before. He had been one of the convention delegates who supported me when I ran for the state legislature.

As I explained the purpose of the angel, the sculptor's eyes began to tear up. He left the room, then returned with the bronze plaque he had made for their own child's headstone. Hyrum Ortho had died eighteen hours after his birth. The plaque was a duplicate of the one that was mounted on their child's headstone nearly three thousand miles away in Laie, Hawaii. They too had no place to go to mourn their child.

Myrna spoke for both of them. "Don't worry about the cost or the deadline. Whatever it takes to build this will be done."

◆

I felt strongly that the new statue, like the original, was to be placed in the Salt Lake City Cemetery. I called the cemetery and explained my intentions to the sexton's secretary. She asked that I send a written request. I sent a letter, including with it a copy of *The Christmas Box*. The next time we spoke she was excited about the prospect of the angel statue. She had read the book and understood the need for the angel. She too had lost a child.

"You'll have to meet with Mr. Byron, the sexton," she said. "He's out of town for the week. If you can call back next Thursday, I'll arrange a meeting."

The following Thursday I called her back.

"There's a problem, Richard," she said.

"What's wrong?"

"You'll just have to talk to Mr. Byron. He's available to meet with you tomorrow."

From the tone of her voice I knew that my request had been denied.

The next day, as I drove up to the cemetery, I contemplated my anticipated rejection and wondered if an appeal was possible. For the first time I began to wonder if the angel would ever stand in the cemetery. Then I said out loud, "How will I even know where it should be?" Suddenly there came to my mind a strong impression: *The place has been chosen.* Doubt quickly replaced the impression. *They're not even going to let me build it,* I thought.

The impression came again: *The place has been chosen.*

◆

The sexton's secretary greeted me, then introduced me to the sexton, who was mulling through paperwork at a cluttered desk. He glanced up. "Just a minute," he said, returning to his work. Paul Byron had worked at the Salt Lake City Cemetery for fifteen years. He knew the place like his own backyard. It was, in fact, his own backyard, for he lived in the house on the property.

He glanced up. "I've heard your request, Mr. Evans, and I'm going to have to deny it."

Despite the secretary's warning, his response still came as a surprise.

"May I ask why?"

He sat back in his chair. "I get a lot of requests like yours and I just can't do it. In the first place this would have to be approved by a half dozen city organizations, including the city council, probably even the mayor. The red tape is considerable. It couldn't possibly be done by this fall, even if I had the time to go to that much trouble, which, frankly,

I don't. Besides, there's no place to put a monument. This cemetery is almost a hundred and fifty years old. The plots are all privately owned. We just don't have the space. I'm sorry."

Then the sexton returned to his paperwork. I just sat there, my mind reeling. I thought I had received inspiration. Not knowing what to do, I did nothing. After a few minutes the sexton looked back up, probably wondering why I was still in his office. "What is it that you're *really* trying to do, Mr. Evans?" he asked.

I looked down for a moment, then back into his eyes. "I just want to build a place where people can go to be healed."

◆

I may never fully understand what happened next. The sexton's countenance suddenly changed. He stood up, walked over to a map on the wall, then, with a pen, made an **X** near the center of the cemetery. "Here," he said. "We could put it here."

We drove up to the site—a beautiful knoll that overlooked the city.

The sexton walked to the crest of the small hill and extended his arms outward, like angel wings. "It will go right here." He looked around. "You'll need more than one plot, though. You'll need at least five. I could write an ordinance that would restrict other grave markers on this hill."

He looked at me thoughtfully. "It's the strangest thing. There's been a utility shed on this property for the last forty years. A few months ago it was torn down. I was supposed to sell the land, I even had buyers, but for some reason I couldn't bring myself to do it." He suddenly turned to me, seemingly as surprised at what he was saying as I was. "People will come from all over the world to see this angel."

As we drove back to the office he said, "I get a lot of requests for this sort of thing and I have always turned them down. I don't know why, but this angel of yours is supposed to be here."

I drove him back to his office. His secretary followed me out to my car.

"What did he say?"

"He's going to allow it. In fact, he's going to request that the city donate the land."

She looked at me incredulously. "Paul said that?"

I nodded.

"It's a miracle," she said.

◆

We set the date of the angel's dedication for December 6, the day of Andrea's death in *The Christmas Box*. I'm often asked why I chose the sixth. No reason, really. I suppose it's just what came to mind.

Ortho and Jared Fairbanks worked long days, often late into the night, to meet the nearly impossible deadline. They delivered the completed sculpture to the bronze foundry only a few weeks before the dedication ceremony. When Ortho went to the foundry to check on the sculpture's progress he was asked by one of the foundry workers if there was something mystical about the angel.

"There are strange things happening with it," he said. "It's come together in a fraction of the time it should have, and several of our workers say they've had unexplainable feelings while working on it. We've begun to call it 'the miracle angel.' "

I planned to pay for the bronze casting with profits from my book. In the meantime I had a lot of books to sell.

22

◆

THE ROAD

It is often during the worst of times that we see the best of humanity—awakening within the most ordinary of us that which is most sublime. I do not believe that it is the circumstance that produces such greatness any more than it is the canvas that makes the artist. Adversity merely presents the surface on which we render our souls' most exacting likeness. It is in the darkest skies that stars are best seen.

THE LETTER

$\mathcal{F}$OR THE NEXT EIGHT WEEKS
I established a book tour routine. I would fly into a city, rent a car and reserve a room at the cheapest hotel near the airport. Then I would do one or two signings and, if lucky, an interview with a local radio station.

I would also stop at nearly every bookstore I drove past. I would go all day, to the point of exhaustion, sometimes parking along the side of the road to nap in the car. I was stopped twice by police for nothing more than looking suspicious. One Dallas patrolman pulled me over because my license plate registration sticker was askew. I pointed out to him that I was driving a rental car, a fact that did not interest him in the least. As he inspected my car I put my hands in my pockets.

"What's in your pocket?" he asked.

"Nothing. I was just putting my hands in my pockets."

"What's in your pocket?" he repeated, his hand now hovering near his gun.

"Nothing. My keys. That's it. Really."

"Raise your hands slowly and put them on top of the car," he shouted, his voice slightly quivering.

I did as he said. He cautiously approached me, then frisked me for weapons. Finding nothing but keys, he reprimanded me for the way the rental company had positioned the car's registration sticker, then left. I wondered if all Texas patrolmen were so pleasant.

I often wondered the same of the bookstores. With a few notable exceptions, the bookstores I visited offered little or no encouragement. Sometimes they couldn't even muster common courtesy. At one book signing in San Diego, the manager acted annoyed by my presence. When I arrived, she hastily grabbed a chair and a stack of my books, both of which she placed in the middle of the store next to a table crowded with other authors' books. People had to squeeze by me all night. I sold only one copy.

As humiliating as those early days were, I had more to worry about than ego. Keri and I had put all our money and our business on the line. And things weren't going well.

A bookstore owner had warned me that even though things had gone well locally, I could not succeed nationally. I soon learned why. It's one thing to get a chain of bookstores to buy your book, it's something else to get the stores to sell it.

As I traveled the country from rental car to Motel 6, I found that outside Utah, not a single bookstore I visited recognized or cared about my book. In many cases they had not even bothered to take my book out of their back room. While it seemed inexcusable to me, it was understandable. Around Christmastime the back rooms of bookstores become cardboard jungles, with boxes of books stacked to the ceiling. With fifty to a hundred thousand different titles, it's easy to get lost in the crowd.

Here and there a ray of hope broke through my gathering clouds of anxiety. Bookstores in Utah and Idaho were selling *The Christmas Box* at even higher levels than the year before. One book catalogue, from the Chinaberry company, reported that *The Christmas Box* was their bestselling item, and a newspaper article in Fort Wayne, Indiana, said that my book had taken their community by storm and become the number-one-selling book in the city. But these were the exceptions, not the rule, and in most places my books were still sitting in unopened boxes. By mid-November I realized just how serious the situation was. If circumstances did not change dramatically I could expect massive returns and would end up with a warehouse full of my unsold books.

And huge debts. Even though we had managed to ship out a lot of books, it meant little. The book industry operates on consignment. If a book does not sell, it is returned to the publisher for credit. Moreover, bookstores would never reorder the book, as their computers would pull up the book's history and report that it didn't sell. It didn't matter that the book was buried somewhere in their back room.

The only thing that could save me was sales. Lots of them.

In addition to my book worries, I had other fears. After years of infertility treatments, Keri was now seven months pregnant with our third child and having a difficult pregnancy. Her doctor had put her on strict bed rest until the baby was ready to be delivered. In dark thoughts I feared a terrible irony—I was speaking daily with people who had lost children through stillbirth or miscarriage, and we were now facing the possibility of losing ours.

Despite the gravity of our situation, the doctor had reassured us that with bed rest Keri and the baby would be fine. And we still had cause to be hopeful about the book. *People* magazine had shown interest in my story and had already sent a photographer out to Salt Lake City for a photo shoot with my family. The photographer had spent a half day shooting pictures of me with my daughters sleigh riding.

I had also landed one national TV appearance. Or at least a national cable appearance—a full fifteen-minute segment with live call-ins on *What's New* at America's Talking.

As the days ticked off toward Christmas our anxiety

grew. I had been initially told that the *People* article would run the week after Thanksgiving, but it didn't. Then another week passed without it. I began to realize that my story might not run. That left us just one hope, the cable TV show. Without it all would be lost.

23

◆

THE
ANGEL
STATUE

$\mathcal{D}$URING THESE WEEKS ONE thing did go right. On December 6 we dedicated the Christmas Box Angel statue in the Salt Lake City Cemetery. The statue had been completed by the foundry and placed upon its granite pedestal just the day before the dedication.

On the day of the dedication ceremony the weather turned inclement. Then, that evening, as Keri and I got ready for the ceremony, it began to rain. It does not often rain in Utah in December. It snows. Utahns are used to snow—they practically relish it. But no one goes out in winter rain. I was angry at first. *Haven't these people suffered enough, God?* I thought. I did not believe anyone would come to the ceremony.

An hour before the event, as darkness fell, cars began to arrive. They came sporadically at first, then they came more steadily, until a long line of cars snaked through the cemetery, visible only by their headlights. It reminded me of the final scene of the movie *Field of Dreams. If you build it, they will come.* That night hundreds of grieving parents braved the elements to attend the statue's dedication.

Among those parents was a woman named Joyce Williams. Joyce had driven from Idaho to attend the ceremony, bearing two hundred long-stem white roses that she handed out to anyone who did not have a flower to lay.

Joyce shared her story with me. More than twenty-five years ago their only son, a two-and-a-half-year-old boy named Robbie, was killed in a tragic farming accident, beneath a tractor being driven by her husband. For all those years he held his pain inside, refusing to share his feelings or hurt. Then, one day, as they drove to visit their daughter, they listened to a radio interview of me talking about *The Christmas Box.* To Joyce's surprise her husband became very interested. He told Joyce that he wanted a copy of the book. They stopped in a bookstore for a copy but no one had heard of it. As she turned to leave, a small green book caught her eye. It was *The Christmas Box.* They brought it home and they took turns reading it. For the first time in more than two decades, he began to speak of their son and the tremendous pain he carried over his loss. His healing had finally begun.

The ceremony that night was simple. A neighborhood children's choir sang Brahms's "Lullaby." I gave a dedicatory prayer, reminding those in attendance that while the earth beneath this statue held no child, no cemetery holds a child, for in God all children live. I also told them that the angel was not to be worshiped or idolized. It was just bronze. The healing could come only from God and the love and support of one another. As strangers huddled together for warmth, I realized that the weather was perfect for the event. These people had endured a much greater storm than could be delivered by clouds. And the way through such storms was to hold to one another for warmth and strength. God knew what he was doing after all.

Near the end of the evening a woman said something to me that truly summed up the event. "Thank you," she said, wiping away her tears. "Finally someone has said it's okay to cry."

That night my father presented me with a wooden box that he had handcrafted from burled walnut, patterned after the box I described in *The Christmas Box.*

Joyce Williams called me the day after the ceremony. That night she had planned to stay in Salt Lake City, but with so much on her mind, she decided instead to make the long drive home to Idaho. A few hours before arriving home, her car tape player broke. She had been listening to a Kenny G tape called *Miracles.*

She fussed with her tape player for some time as she drove, then eventually gave up on it, finishing her ride in silence. She arrived in her city around 2 A.M. In spite of the hour, she decided to stop and visit her son's burial spot.

The ground of the cemetery was lit with newly fallen snow and all the headstones were covered with powder. All except for her son's. She thought this curious, and as she stared silently at her son's grave, the tape in her car suddenly began to play. The song it played was Brahms's "Lullaby," the same song the children had sung at the angel dedication. She bowed her head and wept.

Dear Richard,

Thank you for the beautiful story, The Christmas Box. My son Ben died three years ago, so, you see, this story holds a deeper meaning for me.

This morning I received a gift from a dear friend—your book, a white flower and a crystal angel. I immediately sat down and read The Christmas Box and wept for the pain of my loss, the joy of the gift and the delight of the message it brought me. I felt comforted and full of hope in being reminded that one day I will be able to hold my child again.

I have ordered flowers to be delivered to the statue dedication at the cemetery in Salt Lake City.

Most sincerely,

Sue

Dear Mr. Evans,

I have just finished reading The Christmas Box for the second time. I'm sure I will read it many more times. I would like to thank you for writing this book. It is now my favorite book and I have given copies to special friends because I think the story is so important—especially to people like myself, who have had children die.

My daughter Julie died August 25 at the age of 17. My baby daughter, Clara, died the next evening. I was six months pregnant with her.

After Julie died, a lot of unusual things happened and still do. Julie was always a caregiver. She would drop important work if someone else needed her. I know she is even more of the savior now that she is not of this world.

In 1995 I started seeing your book everywhere I went and kept hearing her tell me I needed to read it. One day I had been especially bothered by her guiding me to the book, but I still didn't buy it. I'm not sure why I resisted it so. But I went home and opened my mail. There was a package from the leader of my Compassionate Friends group. When I opened it, there was a copy of the book. I knew I had to read it immediately.

Like the angel in The Christmas Box, I believe my Julie also plays a music box for me. It is one that must be hand wound in order to play—it can't just get jarred into playing—yet in the middle of the night, just as in The Christmas Box, it often plays.

Sincerely,

Mary H. Harrington

24

◆

THE GREATEST MOMENT

There are moments, it would seem, that were created in cosmic theater where we are given strange and fantastic tests. In these times, we do not show who we are to God, for surely He must already know, but rather to ourselves.

TIMEPIECE

$\mathcal{O}$N NOVEMBER 30 I FLEW
to New Jersey for my cable appearance, arriving at the
Newark airport around 1 A.M. I got up early the next morning for the show, taking a taxi across the New Jersey Turn-
pike into Manhattan. A young woman came out to greet
me in the lobby.

"What's with the big bag?" she asked.

I had brought my suitcase filled with clothes. "I brought
a few extra outfits in case you wanted me to change what I
was wearing."

"You won't be on long enough for it to really matter."

I wondered what she meant by that as she led me to a
crowded greenroom. After a while she returned for me and
we stopped in the hallway as she introduced me to the
show's producer—a thin, Jim Carrey look-alike about my
age.

"You're the Christmas story guy," he said. "Sorry we had
to cut your segment."

"What?"

"We have this really funny segment with this snore-cure product. We taped one of our cameramen sleeping last night. It's really great."

I wasn't amused.

"Sorry, man. No one told you?"

"No. I just flew all the way from Salt Lake."

He frowned. "We have a little time during the cooking segment. We could squeeze in a half minute. It would at least give you a chance to hold up your book."

I did. It was a waste of time. The host asked me about my book as he stood behind a table sampling bourbon bonbons. I was gone with the commercial break.

As everyone ran off to prepare for the next segment, I unclipped my microphone.

"May I stay and watch the rest of the taping?" I asked the assistant.

"Why?" she asked curtly.

I handed her the microphone and walked out. I retrieved my suitcase and carried it to the lobby. "May I use your phone?" I asked the receptionist.

"Local, or long distance?"

"I just need to call a taxi."

"All right," she said grudgingly.

I waited in the parking lot for the cab. When I arrived at the hotel I went up to my room and called Keri. It was good to hear her voice.

"How'd it go?" she asked.

"Did you see it?"

"I couldn't find it on TV."

"It's just as well. They pretty much canceled my segment."

Uneasy silence. "Why?"

"They had some snore product."

More silence.

"How are you?" I asked.

"I'm okay. Just being a good girl and staying down. How are you?"

"I'm pretty bummed. But there's still *People* magazine."

"Where are you calling from?"

"Newark. I fly to Atlanta in a couple of hours."

"Call me from there."

"All right. I love you."

"Love you too."

I arrived in Atlanta late that afternoon. My first book signing was at a Waldenbooks in Duluth. The manager was bright and enthusiastic. She had not only read my book but had bought a half dozen copies for Christmas gifts. She did much to lift my spirits. I needed it.

The next day, Saturday, ten minutes to one, I arrived at another bookstore, this one at a mall in Alpharetta, Georgia. The store was quiet and there was only one employee visible, a young, dishwater blond woman, standing behind a cash register at the front counter. There was no table for signing books and no signs announcing my book signing. I approached the woman. "Hi, I'm Richard Paul Evans. I'm here for my book signing."

She looked at me quizzically. "What signing?"

"The one I came from Salt Lake City for," I replied.

"We don't have a signing today," she insisted.

"Is your manager here?"

"He just left. What book did you write?"

"It's called *The Christmas Box*."

"Never heard of it," she said. "I don't know if we sell it."

"May I use your phone?"

"There's one in the back room."

I went to the back of the store, plying my way between the stacked boxes and wondering if my book was buried beneath the cardboard mountains. I called Mike at the distributor's.

"Where are you?" he asked.

"In Georgia. I just arrived for my signing. They say they don't have a signing today."

"The manager said that?"

"The manager's not here."

"I'll call the buyer," he said. I gave him the store phone number and hung up. He called back about five minutes later.

"Your signing was set," Mike said. "The buyer thinks the manager screwed up. That's probably why he's not there. He's hiding."

"Great."

"Sorry. It happens. How did the cable show go?"

"Bad. They pretty much cut my segment."

"Figures. We didn't see any increase in sales."

"I didn't think you would."

He sighed. "You're not having a real good week. Especially with what happened to *People* magazine."

My heart froze. "What happened to *People*?"

"Oh," he said, unaware that I didn't know. "You didn't hear. Your office was probably waiting for you to get back. *People* canceled your article."

"Canceled?"

"Yeah. I'm sorry."

"But why?"

"They don't believe it. Seems no one in New York has heard of you."

"Tell them to call the booksellers."

"They did. They confirmed your story, but I guess they'd already made up their minds."

I hung up the phone. I was numb. I walked back to the front counter. The woman was helping a customer. She turned toward me. "Hey, I found your books. They were under the counter. There's only eleven of them."

"Want me to sign them?"

"No," she said, returning to her register. "You can just go."

I left the store. It had begun to rain. I walked out to my

rented Pontiac Grand Prix, put the keys in the ignition, then just sat inside while the rain pounded on the roof and hood. I was filled with tremendous despair—despair that evolved into anger. "God," I said bitterly, "you've given me just enough rope to hang myself."

What happened next I cannot adequately describe. Instantly a powerful, external force shaped words in my mind.

Why did you write this book? it asked.

I didn't answer.

Did you do it for the money?

I thought for a moment. "I wrote the book for my daughters. I wasn't even going to publish it. It was never about money. But now I'm broke."

Did you do it for your pride?

This was more difficult to answer. "Not at first. I thought this book was helping people. But I don't like looking like a fool."

Do you believe that this book was given to you?

"Yes," I replied.

Then I will do with this book as I will.

Reality sunk in. I realized my quest was really over and I had lost. I would pay dearly for dreaming. Yet some vestige of faith and trust in God, no doubt planted and nurtured by my parents in my youth, spoke back to that "voice" what might be the most difficult words in any language to speak: "Thy will be done."

As I flew home that night all I could think about was Keri. She had believed in me when I shut down my business and invested our savings. How could I tell her that we were going to have to start all over? The doctor had told her to avoid stress, and here I was the carrier of the darkest news of all. How could I tell her? How *would* I tell her? The only thing I was certain of was that I would wait until morning.

I arrived in Salt Lake City around 2 A.M. It had snowed while I was gone and the airport parking lot was concealed beneath a blanket of snow. It took me a half hour to find my car and another ten minutes to unbury it. It was nearly three by the time I arrived home. As I opened our bedroom door I could hear Keri's breathing. I undressed in the hallway and stepped inside with the lights off, hoping not to wake her.

"Welcome home, honey," she said sleepily.

"Hi."

"You didn't call. How'd it go in Atlanta?"

I stood at the edge of the bed. "Not too good."

"What happened?"

"The bookstore manager forgot I was coming." I hesitated. "Honey, I got a call from Mike Hurst. *People* magazine canceled. We're going to lose a lot of money."

The words hung in the quiet room and that short moment of silence seemed stretched into agonizing minutes.

Then from the darkness came Keri's soft voice. "But think of all the good you've done."

This was a moment I will cherish for the rest of my life. In that dark moment in the middle of the night I climbed into bed thinking, *I'm a lucky man.*

25

♦

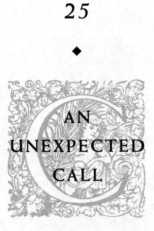

AN UNEXPECTED CALL

Even the most horrible of nightmares is laced with the promise of dawn.

THE LOCKET

$\mathcal{E}$VEN THOUGH I WAS WITH-
out hope, I was still unwilling to give up without a fight. Or
at least the semblance of one. I spent most of the morning
sitting at my desk thinking, racking my brain for ideas.
Was there any way to beat this? What had I missed? Around ten
o'clock my secretary, Heather, paged me. "Rick, the reporter from *People* is on the line."

"What does she want?" I asked.

"She didn't say."

I lifted the phone.

"Hi, Richard. This is Cathy. I just wanted to verify how
many copies of your book you've shipped to date."

"What does it matter?" I said. "There's no story."

"Well, there's been a change. The editor decided last
night to go with the piece after all. Your story will be in the
next issue."

Early Sunday morning I drove to the nearest grocery
store. The new week's magazines had not been brought
out yet and when I told a stock boy that I was supposed to

be in *People*, he went into the back and brought out a stack of magazines still bound together with a plastic band. He cut them open. I pawed through the magazine until I found it—a full-page article with a large picture of my two daughters and me riding a sled, all beneath the headline A CHRISTMAS TREASURE. I stared at the page in disbelief.

"That's you," the stock boy said. "Hey," he shouted to a guy standing behind a register, "this guy's in *People* magazine."

◆

Monday morning the distributor was flooded with calls from around the country. I spoke that morning at a local middle school and as I left the school I turned my cell phone on. It rang almost immediately.

"Rick, this is Heather," she said frantically. "I've been trying to reach you. You need to go home right away."

"What's wrong?"

She could barely restrain herself. "NBC just called. They're flying you and the girls out to New York tonight. You're going to be on the *Today* show tomorrow morning with Katie Couric!"

I screamed. "Does Keri know?"

"Are you kidding? She's out shopping for new Christmas dresses for the girls."

"She's out of bed?"

"I don't think chains could have kept her down."

Allyson, Jenna and I flew out at 5 P.M. and arrived in New York around midnight. As I walked from the plane a uniformed driver stood near the Jetway exit. He held a sign that read, *Richard Paul Evans.* He saw me glance at the sign. "Are you Mr. Evans?"

"Yes, I am," I said, proud to be me for the first time in months.

It was our first time in a stretch limousine. NBC put us up in a spacious suite across from New York's Central Park. Our room was bigger than the upstairs of my home. At least it had more bathrooms. Three of them. I put the girls to bed, then set the alarm and did not fall asleep until past two. My mind would not stop. *How did I get here?*

I slept only a few hours, got up early the next morning, woke the girls and got them dressed. I realized then that we hadn't packed Jenna's dress shoes. She would have to go on the show shoeless. She put on her sneakers with her dress. Then I did the best that I could with their hair, meaning that it was a disaster.

"I hope there's someone who can do hair," I said to Jenna.

"Me too," Jenna agreed.

We ordered one Continental breakfast. It was all I could justify paying for. "Four dollars for a glass of orange juice," I said to the girls. "We'll share."

We went down to the hotel lobby, where our limousine

driver was waiting. We were driven just a few blocks to the studio and taken to the greenroom.

Considering my last greenroom experience I was more than a little anxious. On the couch opposite me was a young Asian woman dressed in what looked like a tin-soldier costume. The woman's mother came over and talked to my girls, complimenting me on how pretty they were. It was not until we saw the young woman on the monitor that we realized it was Olympic gold medalist Kristi Yamaguchi. She was ice-skating in the Rockefeller Center ice rink.

"Dad!" Jenna said, "I have a poster of Kristi on my door and I didn't even know it was her!"

Thankfully there was food in the greenroom, a tray of fruit and pastries, and there *was* someone there who could do hair and makeup. My daughters charmed the NBC staff and everyone doted over them. As I was coming back from makeup, the elevator door at the end of the hallway opened.

"Out of the hall," someone shouted. Katie Couric and Bryant Gumbel were returning to the studio after interviewing Kristi. With no place to go I stood up against the wall. Just then Bryant passed by me, followed by Katie. Starstruck, I watched them pass. Then Katie stopped and turned back toward me. "Are you Richard?" she asked.

I nodded, astonished at how pretty she was in real life and even more astonished that she had acknowledged my existence. She smiled. "Don't worry about a thing, we're going to have a good time. You have a great story. I'll see you in a few minutes."

From the greenroom monitor we watched Katie introduce my segment. "When we come back we'll meet a Salt Lake City man who wrote a book for his two daughters, and now it's a bestseller."

Bryant said, "Is that the guy we almost ran over in the hall?"

Katie laughed. "That's Richard . . ."

◆

A minute later I was escorted downstairs with my girls for the interview. The interview went well, but it was my girls who stole the show. Allyson, who was only five years old at the time, could see herself in the studio monitor and giggled every time the camera was on her. The cameramen loved it and played up to her with a lot of close-ups. I was later told that the NBC switchboards were flooded with calls from approving viewers.

There was one near disaster. Allyson was inches away from picking her nose in front of millions of viewers. Katie saw it coming and diverted the action by asking her a question. Allyson's hand dropped.

Then it was over. Katie thanked me for coming, then walked back up to the set as I herded my girls to the side of the studio. Still shell-shocked from my last television appearance, I hesitantly asked our escort if we could watch the rest of the taping.

"Of course," she said, smiling.

"Do you think I could get a picture of Katie and Bryant?"

She smiled again. "Of course."

Katie and Bryant were taping I.D. tags for local television stations when Katie suddenly stood up. "Come on, Bryant, I'm tired of this. Let's take pictures with Richard and his girls."

After a series of shots (including several that Katie took herself), Katie said, "Richard, have you taken your girls to FAO Schwarz?"

"I don't know what that is."

"Did you see the movie *Big* with Tom Hanks?"

I nodded.

"It's the toy store in the movie. It's right on Fifth Avenue. Your daughters will love it." Katie motioned to one of the assistants. "Would you please show Richard the way to FAO Schwarz, then arrange to have a car pick him and his girls up?"

◆

People often ask me what Katie Couric is *really* like, as if I saw something off camera that might shed light on her *real* personality. I think I did meet the real Katie Couric. I saw that she's a skilled interviewer and a kind, genuine person. And though it was just another day at work for her, it was a day I'll never forget.

Nor will my daughters. We were on vacation a year later when Allyson asked if she could buy a postcard for her friend Katie. Only when she asked me to help her with the address did I realize that she was talking about Katie Couric.

We said good-bye to Bryant and Katie, and our escort walked us over to Fifth Avenue, then up several blocks. "You're just about there. Just keep walking straight, it's four or five blocks ahead on the other side of the street. You'll see it."

Back then I did not trust Manhattan. A few years earlier a young Utah man had been stabbed to death in the New York subway while protecting his mother from a gang robbery. Even though the family of the young man had thanked New Yorkers for their compassion and sympathy, it pretty much confirmed most Utahns' perception of New York as a heartless, crime-ridden city.

As we walked, I huddled my girls in close. We had walked only one block when a woman, shabbily dressed, glanced at me and began walking toward us. I avoided eye contact until it was clear that she was coming directly at me.

"Excuse me, sir."

I pulled my girls close.

"I saw you and your little girls this morning on the *Today* show. I just wanted to tell you that I thought what you had to say was really beautiful. We need more people like you in this world."

Three other New Yorkers stopped us that morning with similar comments.

Dear Mr. Evans,

My name is Sharon Dalton. I am thirty-four years old and I have two-year-old girl triplets. On August 1 of last year, my husband passed away unexpectedly.

This Christmas is very difficult for me because of the loss of my husband. I am writing this letter to you because I have just finished reading The Christmas Box and I want you to know what great comfort your book has given to me on this first Christmas my children and I will have without Dan. I thank God for my three angels. Your book has helped me to try to think of how blessed I am to have their love. I know that Christmastime will never feel the same for me but your book has helped me to view Christmas through the eyes of my three beautiful angels.

To paraphrase your book, "Though the cold winds of life have put a frost on my heart, the love I have surrounding me will shelter my heart from life's storms."

Thank you for writing.

Merry Christmas,

Sharon

◆

26

BACK
AT THE
RANCH

$\mathcal{T}$HE GIRLS AND I FLEW home that same day, arriving in Salt Lake City around 7 P.M. My brother-in-law, Wally, who works for Delta Airlines, met us at the airport and took the girls home while I drove off to a speaking event I had promised to do for my publicist. I suppose I was a bit distracted by the day's events, as it had snowed all day in Utah and the freeway looked more like tundra than asphalt. And I was driving as if I hadn't noticed.

Coming around a bend in the freeway I turned the wheel only to find that my car did not respond. I glanced down at the speedometer. I was traveling nearly sixty miles per hour, completely out of control. The car maintained for a few hundred feet, then it began to slide sideways off the road. My first thought was that I was glad the girls were not with me. Then I thought, *How strange that I would have two surreal experiences in one day. A* Today *show appearance in the morning and death at night.*

My car went over the side of the highway, missing several light posts and plowing into a high bank of snow, burying my car in the powder. I must have created a tremendous flume of white, as within moments another motorist pulled over to help me. I walked from the accident without a scratch, grateful to be safe, and angry at my carelessness. It was the first time I had missed a speaking engagement.

◆

The next morning I called my distributor. Their phones and fax machine had not stopped since my television appearance, and by the time they arrived at work that morning a pile of fax orders had collected on the ground. The orders and reorders for my book were already in the tens of thousands, and that week Publishers Distribution Center shipped out an additional seventy thousand copies.

I later learned from bookstore managers that the morning of our *Today* show appearance, people lined up outside bookstores all across America to buy my book.

As in the year before, demand for *The Christmas Box* continued to increase. My distributor had to hire extra employees to assist in shipping.

The Wednesday before Christmas I was in a shopping mall parking terrace when I received a phone call from my secretary, Heather. "Some man just called," she said. "I think he said he was from Dell Publishing. Some big publishing house. He said that the *New York Times* advance report just came out and he wanted to congratulate you because *The Christmas Box* just hit the *New York Times* bestseller list."

Despite the fact that *The Christmas Box* was in less than one out of five bookstores in America, one week after the phone call it debuted at number two on the *New York Times* paperback bestseller list.

27

◆

THE
BOOK
WORLD

$\mathcal{T}$HE DAY MY BOOK HIT THE list, publishers decided they really did want my book after all. The calls began to come. In addition to the publisher calls, I was receiving about three movie calls a day. I had already optioned the motion picture rights to a local company that eventually inked a deal with CBS. *The Christmas Box* was made into a holiday special starring Maureen O'Hara and Richard Thomas. It went on to win an Emmy and to be the highest-rated television movie of 1995.

The fifth publishing house to call made an offer. "I'm authorized to offer you two million dollars right now for the hardcover and paperback rights to your book," he said.

"Two million dollars," I repeated.

"We don't want to mess around with an auction."

I had never before heard of a book auction. "I'm not selling the paperback rights," I said.

"Why?"

"Because I can't," I replied.

"Why?" he repeated.

"Because I had a feeling that I'm not supposed to sell them."

A few days earlier as I was meditating on my book I had had an impression that I was not to sell the paperback rights. And that I was to bring the inexpensive paperback version out at the same time as the hardcover. I knew I was giving the book away and I didn't doubt that I would lose money by doing so, but making money wasn't the point. Everyone was supposed to be able to afford this book.

"No publisher will buy your book if you don't sell the paperback rights," he said.

"No publisher wanted it before," I said.

Frustrated, he wished me luck and said good-bye. He called back the next day.

"One million dollars and you keep the paperback rights."

"I need some time to think about it," I said. "I've been on the road for several months and I'm tired. My wife's going to have a baby in a few days."

"I understand. Congratulations," he said. "About the baby as well as the book."

"Thanks. I'm also looking for an agent."

"Do you have one in mind?"

"No. But there are several calling."

"I bet," he said.

◆

The next day the doorbell rang. A man held one of the largest flower bouquets I had ever seen. I read the note. *Congratulations on the new baby. Simon & Schuster.*

It was the first of the flood to come. After two days, our dining room and kitchen were filled with flowers until our house looked more like a funeral parlor than a home. At one point the doorbell rang and Keri said, "Oh no, not more flowers."

"Probably are," I said.

"How long do you think this will keep up?"

"Until I sign with one of them."

◆

Abigail Hope was born January 3. Mother and child were both fine. After another week of avoiding calls I started the task of finding an agent.

◆

Choosing an agent was more difficult than I imagined. I spoke to every agent who called, made what I believed was an informed choice, then knelt down to pray for a confirmation. To my surprise a different name came to mind than the one I had chosen. *Laurie Liss.*

I was puzzled. Even though Laurie Liss had a few years previously discovered a little book called *The Bridges of Madison County*, she was the last name on my list of prospective agents. And according to her own agent bio, she specialized in feminist books. But like previous inspirations, it would not let go. After several days, I reluctantly agreed to meet with her. She flew into Salt Lake to meet with me.

Laurie did not look the way I thought an agent should look. She was my age, small, slender, with graying hair and stylish glasses that made her look older than she really was.

"I loved your book," she said. "It touched a quiet place in my heart. I believe there is something very special about it."

It was a good opening line. But I was waiting for her to compare my book to *The Bridges of Madison County*, a book that, at its core, is about adultery.

"I felt the same way when I first read *The Bridges of Madison County* . . ."

Here it comes, I thought.

". . . except that *Bridges* was about adultery. Your book is about the best within us. It's about loving our children and caring for each other."

Within moments Laurie was telling me everything I believed about my book. Either she was reading my mind or she understood my vision, I thought. By the time she boarded the plane to return to New York I knew she was the right agent. But I didn't want to admit it. It took me two days to call her. "Congratulations," I said, "you have a new author."

"Congratulations yourself," she replied, "you have a damn good agent."

Laurie called all the publishers who had called me, as well as a few others, and announced an auction. With an offer already on the table for a million dollars, she told them to "open their checkbooks to seven figures."

I flew into New York and Laurie met me at the airport. Early the next morning we began meeting with publishers. I learned that I knew nothing about the publishing establishment. As we walked out of the first meeting I said, "I think we should just meet with large publishers."

Laurie smiled. "St. Martin's is a very large publisher," she replied.

After two days of meetings I flew home. The last thing Laurie said to me was, "Don't talk to anyone but me."

The next morning I received a phone call around ten o'clock mountain time.

"Round one is over," Laurie said.

"What are we at?"

"Are you sitting down?" she asked with mock drama. I sat down.

"Two and three-quarter million."

For a moment I was speechless. Then I asked, "Are you kidding?"

"Nope."

"Did everyone else drop out?"

"Only two publishers. This is going on for days."

The auction went on for two and a half days, at the end of which Simon & Schuster paid more than 4 million dollars for North American hardcover rights. I suppose it was like winning the lottery. But that was the kind of thing that only happened to someone else.

28

◆

THE OTHER SIDE OF THE BANK

Gold is an able servant but a cruel master.

THE LOOKING GLASS

$\mathcal{T}$HE FIRST INSTALLMENT from my publishing contract came in April. When the check arrived my younger brother, Barry, who had come to work for me, brought it into my office. For a moment we both just sat and stared at it.

"You ever see a check that big?" Barry asked.

"No. Definitely not with my name on it."

"What are you going to do with it?"

"Put it in the bank."

I faxed a copy of the check to a few of my friends (they had asked to see it), then Barry and I went to our bank. I walked up to the teller and handed her the check. "I'll need some cash back," I said.

For a moment she just stared at the check. Then she said, "I think you need to see someone else about this."

She led us over to a man sitting at a desk. Barry and I sat down in the chairs in front of him.

"What seems to be the problem?" he asked.

"I was just trying to deposit this check and I asked for

some cash back." I handed him the check. I saw the surprise on his face. "Just a moment," he said, and he left the room. About five minutes later he returned, followed by a tall, smiling man.

"Mr. Evans," he said, "what a pleasure. I'm sorry for the inconvenience. You're on the wrong side of the bank."

Barry and I looked at each other. We didn't know there was another side. The smiling man led us over to the promised land of banking services. On the other side of the bank everyone knew who I was. Everyone seemed much happier over there. And there were little dishes of candy at every desk.

29

◆

A HOME FOR CHILDREN

How quickly it is forgotten that Midas's gift was a curse, not a blessing.

THE LOOKING GLASS

$\mathcal{A}$ FEW DAYS LATER KERI and I sat in our white minivan in the parking lot outside a financial consultant's office. The meeting we had just endured was not what we had expected. We had talked for nearly two hours about trust funds and portfolios, the problems of wealth and how to shield our children from the money should they become drug addicts and alcoholics. The well-meaning advisers, in an effort to help us protect our funds, shared story after story of families broken by wealth. My mother was always worried about the effect of money on her children. It was a trait I would likewise carry. In an interview with the *New York Times*, my agent said, "I've never seen anyone so nervous about money as Rick."

Now Keri was worried as well.

"Not exactly what I expected," I said.

Keri looked at me seriously. "Maybe we should just give the money back."

This led to a lively discussion. By the time we left the parking lot we had come to the conclusion that our windfall was not inherently good or bad. What mattered was how we chose to use it. We decided that we would not rush out and buy new cars and toys. We would move gradually. And we would teach our children how to use money by helping others. We decided to start a foundation.

I had one other desire. My father was in his sixties and was still doing heavy construction work without any retirement put aside. On several occasions my brothers and I had discussed what we could do to help. I went to my father. "Dad, you can retire now."

His reaction rolled me. "I don't need your money," he said tersely.

In trying to help, I had offended him. Having money was more difficult than I imagined.

A few days later it occurred to me that my father's business experience and master's in social work qualified him to run our foundation. I asked him to come help us spend our money helping children. My father was more than happy to dust off his M.S.W., and to everyone's benefit, he accepted the job.

Every child is worthy of love.

THE LETTER

Once my father was settled in his new position, we sat down to discuss the direction our new foundation would take.

"Keri and I want to help abused children," I said, "but we're not sure how. I think if you look around, the cause might find us."

My father went up to the University of Utah to meet with Dean Kay Dea of the Graduate School of Social Work. "If anyone knows what Utah's children need," my father said, "it's him."

At the dean's suggestion we sponsored a children's advocacy conference, inviting child advocates from around Utah. We asked them directly: *What is the single most important thing we could do to help our abused and neglected children?*

We learned three things from our conference: First, that for the most part these advocates did not communicate with one another. Second, that there are fierce turf wars in the field of child advocacy and these groups did not especially like one another; in fact, we had to seat some of them at different tables. Third, we learned that nearly everyone in attendance was in agreement about what needed to be done to help children.

It was determined that we desperately needed a building, a shelter where a child could be taken twenty-four hours a day, rather than just being thrust into the first home available whether it was an appropriate environment or not.

But more than just a shelter, this facility should be a one-stop mall of children's services, bringing these services to the child in a comfortable setting and encouraging dialogue between different child advocacy groups by putting them under the same roof.

In addition it would become a community resource center, strengthening families and children and drawing support from the community it served through donations and volunteerism.

To maintain the integrity of the foundation that would operate the facility, I committed to pay for all foundation administrative overhead costs from the sales of my books, so all other donations went directly to help the children.

The concept of the Christmas Box House was born.

◆

30

STANDING
ALONE

The premonitions that we so quickly dismiss are sometimes our truest glances of reality.

THE LETTER

$\mathcal{I}$N MARCH I FLEW BACK to New York to meet with my new publisher. We discussed book design and marketing plans. They were amenable to all of my ideas except for one: the paperback release. The afternoon of the second day I was brought into a meeting with the sales managers. It was actually an ambush. The V.P. of sales spoke first.

"You can't publish the paperback," he said. "You'll destroy any chance you have at success."

"I have to," I said.

They all looked at me. "Why?" one of them asked.

"Because I *feel* that I have to."

The sales director tried her luck. "Let me explain this. Fall is the most competitive time of the year for publishers. You'll be competing with the biggest authors and books in the world. By bringing out the paperback at the same time as the hardcover you'll split your sales. It's like playing basketball with Michael Jordan and spotting him points. Your book will never hit a bestseller list. We'll have fewer sells, you'll make less money. It doesn't make sense."

"I know it doesn't make sense," I said, "but I knew going into this that I had to do it this way. So did you. It was part of the deal."

Finally, at an impasse, the V.P. said something I find even more remarkable today than I did then. "You know, nothing about this book has been conventional. If Rick feels that this is the way it's supposed to be, maybe it is."

31

◆

THE MISSION CONTINUES

When I consider the hardships that some must face, my troubles seem foolish and petty—a succession of quixotic battles. To God, perhaps, they are all windmills.

THE LOCKET

$\mathcal{T}$HE CHRISTMAS BOX WAS released by Simon & Schuster in hardcover on October 11. Within a few weeks it hit America's major bestseller lists, including the *New York Times*, the *Wall Street Journal* and *USA Today*.

In early November I arrived in Atlanta and was picked up by a media escort named Lynda. She was attractive and congenial. She commented that she had purchased a dozen copies of my book. This surprised me as she had earlier mentioned that she was Jewish.

"Do you often buy Christmas books?" I asked.

She smiled at the question. "No. But there's something special about your book."

"There is," I said. "Watch what happens today. People will come to my book signing and they won't know why. After I talk to them they'll tell me that they've just lost a child."

I don't know if she believed me. My first signing that

day was at a Sam's Club. We had been there for only a few minutes when a woman wandered up to my table.

"Would you like a book?" I asked.

"No, I guess not. Actually I need something for my sister. She just lost her child."

I talked with the woman for a while and I signed a copy of the book for her sister.

After she left, Lynda said, "That's amazing." A few hours later we dropped by a mall for a "drive-by signing." (That's when you sign the store's stock of your book and meet the bookstore personnel, but avoid the public.) As I signed the last of my books on the front shelf a woman walked up behind me.

"What are you doing?" she asked.

"Signing my book."

"What book is it?"

I held out a copy. "*The Christmas Box.*"

Lynda, being a dutiful escort, quickly said, "Would you like a copy?"

"No, thank you," she said. "Actually, I've been walking the mall for a couple of hours looking for something for my friend. Her little boy was just killed."

I spoke with the woman for a few minutes and she walked away with a book. As we left the store Lynda turned to me.

"Does this really follow you everywhere you go?"

"Yes."

"I don't think I would have believed it if I hadn't seen it with my own eyes. There's no explanation for it."

"I think there is," I said. "I think God loves his children and he has a lot of children that need to be healed."

At another book signing, in Las Vegas, I told the young woman helping me at the table about the phenomenon. Within the hour a woman approached us. "Will this book help someone who has just lost a child?"

I told her about my book and she purchased a copy. After the woman left, the young bookstore employee eyed me curiously, then asked, "Are you real?"

"What do you mean?"

"I mean, are you a real person? Or are you really an angel?"

I smiled. "No, I'm real."

She still looked at me peculiarly.

"Really," I said, "you can ask my wife."

◆

In many respects my second book tour was more difficult than my first. I was the media flavor of the week. *Time*, *Newsweek*, *USA Today*, *Ladies' Home Journal*, *Good Housekeeping*, the *Washington Post*, the *New York Times*, the *Wall Street Journal* and hundreds of other publications had all called for interviews or sent reporters. My publicist had a four-inch stack of media requests on her desk. I was constantly on the road, and even when I was home I was not left alone. During one brief stop in Utah I kissed Jenna good night, then told her I would be leaving again early in the morning. Her eyes watered.

"Dad," she said, "why did you write a book about spending time with your children and now you're leaving again?"

All I could do was hold her.

Dear Richard,

At the request of my wife, I have just finished reading The Christmas Box. *She said it would help me to further appreciate my two-and-a-half-year-old son, Dave.*

I do not think I have ever been so moved by any book or movie as I was by your story.

Toward the end, like Mary, I was in tears. The pages of the book are still moist. My work career takes me out of town often and when I was gone last week, it was particularly painful. I walked into my house, grabbed my wife, Denise, and my son and cried for ten minutes.

I wanted to tell you how much I loved your book. It has helped open my eyes. Your book strengthens my resolve to be at home with my family.

Please give our regards to your family.

All the best,

Dennis

32

◆

SPEAKING

That which we spend our lives hoping for is often no more than another chance to do what we should have done to begin with.

THE LOCKET

IN ADDITION TO MY MEDIA appearances and book signings, I was now giving a lot of speeches as well. Book clubs, churches, fund-raisers, writers' conferences and grief and healing seminars, as well as a dozen other venues. In these settings the miracles and mission of my book became even more evident.

In one instance, after my speech, a woman approached me. Her husband stood next to her with his arm around her. She was wiping tears from her eyes.

"I had never heard of you or your book," she said, "but when I saw in the paper that you were in town I suddenly had an overwhelming feeling that I needed to hear you speak. And that I should wear this . . ." She opened her locket to reveal the picture of her infant daughter. "My baby died."

As I had learned years before from my own experience, there are ways besides death to lose a child. There are those who lose children through their own choices—

those who trade *diamonds for stones*. Both kinds of loss demand grief.

I had just finished speaking to a large group about the importance of spending time with our children when an elderly man walked up toward me. As he neared I noticed his face seemed twisted in anguish. He stepped up on the platform and pointed at me with his forefinger, gesturing with it as he spoke. "You're right, Mr. Evans. You're right. But I'm an old man and I can't go back."

Then he turned and walked away.

Another memorable experience occurred at a church in Baltimore. The morning after my speech, as I was preparing to leave town, a man called.

"Mr. Evans, I was at your speaking event last night. Something happened while you were speaking and I need to talk with you about it. Could we possibly meet for a few minutes?"

"I'd like to," I said, "but I'm about to catch a flight out."

"It's really important. I'll even come to the airport. I just need a couple of minutes. I need to ask you something about last night."

"Can you ask me now?"

"It would be better if we could speak in person."

His earnestness intrigued me. We arranged to meet just minutes before I was to leave for the airport. I was standing near my car, my luggage in tow, when he arrived. He introduced himself, thanked me for my time, then said, "Last night, something happened while you were speaking. You were suddenly completely encompassed in light. At first I didn't believe what I saw and I blinked, then I moved around in my seat. But the light didn't change. It was as if the light emanated from your skin. I turned to my wife and asked her if she saw what I saw, but she didn't say anything. She just sat there listening to you. Then, as you finished speaking, the light gradually diminished until it was gone. Last night I lay in bed for hours just thinking about what I had seen. I thought my wife was asleep, when suddenly she said, 'You saw the light, didn't you?'

"I said, 'You saw it too? Why didn't you say something?' She said it frightened her. She hadn't ever seen anything like it."

The man looked me in the eyes. "What does it mean?"

I asked him when he saw the light. He said it was near the end of my talk, when I had been speaking about our divine life purpose.

"I believe you've been given a sign," I said. "A sign is not a destination, it merely points the way. It's now up to you to learn for yourself whether or not what I said was true."

As we parted I wished him luck on his journey. It was the first time I was to hear about the light. Over the next few years it would become almost commonplace.

◆

Probably my most incredible incident at a speaking event involved a young mother and the Christmas Box Angel statue.

Throughout the year I often visit the angel statue. It's peaceful there. If there is such a thing as holy ground, and I believe there is, I suppose the angel would qualify. Sitting on the grass next to the statue, I would often read the notes and letters that people left to their departed loved ones. A few days after Easter, I came across this note.

My little girl,

I love and miss you very much! Happy Easter. I hope you got a new dress where you are.

I think of you often, especially lately. I will always love you.

Love, Mommy

I brought the note back to my office and put it in the small walnut Christmas Box that my father had made for me. About six months later I was speaking to a large church group about loss and hope. When I was done, a woman came up to speak with me. Her eyes were red from crying.

"I was moved by what you had to say. Your speech also really affected my daughter. She would like to speak with you, but she's having a little trouble. She lost her child last year."

I looked over to see a young woman rubbing her eyes. I walked over to her and she tried to speak, but couldn't. I put my arms around her and held her for a while. Then, still looking down, she said, "Thank you for what you shared tonight. It meant a lot to me. I've been to your angel statue."

Suddenly, in my mind's eye, I saw very clearly the Easter note I had read months earlier. I said, "I know. You left a note for your daughter. It said that you hope there are Easter dresses where she is."

The young woman looked up into my face, her eyes wide with surprise. "How did you know that?"

Her mother looked at me in awe, awaiting my answer.

"I don't know," I said. "I just saw it."

For a moment the three of us shared in the miracle. Then I saw something on the young woman's face that I hadn't before. Hope. I believe that she suddenly understood that if such things could happen, maybe there is more than just this existence. As the two of them walked away, neither of them was crying anymore.

33

◆

PRISON

$\mathcal{I}$ WAS ASKED BY A PRISON chaplain to address a group of inmates at the Utah State Penitentiary. It was a Sunday morning and I arrived about forty-five minutes before I was to speak to allow for security procedures. After passing through a metal detector, I was brought by a guard into a secure room, where I was briefly detained while my clearance was verified. Then I surrendered my I.D. to the guard behind the bulletproof glass for a guest pass. The electric lock on the door buzzed and I walked out into a courtyard.

As I entered in with the prison population I admit I felt a little anxious—a bit like a skin diver leaving a shark cage. I thought of the scripture "I was in prison and you came to me." Someone from the church led me to the chapel and I entered alongside the first group of inmates—men in white cotton jumpsuits stenciled with their prison number and the words *Property of USP.*

I spoke four times that day, as the prison populations could not be mixed. Men and women were brought into different rooms wearing different-color jumpsuits. The men all wore white. The women wore white, red and blue, indicative of their behavior in the facility.

I had been warned that the women inmates would be more difficult than the men. This was true, as my talk to the female inmates was interrupted by catcalls, loud talking and laughter. At least at first. As I spoke to them of the miracles I had witnessed in publishing my book, the women became more attentive. Near the end of my talk all of them were listening and most of them were visibly moved. After I finished, one woman seated several rows back raised her hand.

"I just wanted to say that what Mr. Evans said is true. His book saved my life." Then she sat down, leaving me wondering about her story as the group was ushered from the room to be led away by prison guards.

A week later I received a letter from the prison. It was from the woman who had stood at the end of my talk. She wanted to tell me her story.

She said that the day of the year she hated most was her birthday. Every birthday she received the same thing from her mother—a can of frosting and a box of cake mix. Then her mother would run off to the bar. She would immediately begin looking for a place to take her younger siblings, because she knew that her mother would return drunk and beat them all. It was an annual ritual.

She said that one birthday was worse than she could

have imagined. Her mother brought home two men from the bar. One of them came into her room and raped her repeatedly for seven hours. She was shattered by the experience but never told anyone.

Several months later she learned that she was pregnant. She had used drugs in the past but after the rape she was using them heavily to deal with her emotional pain. When she found out that she was pregnant she stopped using them, but it was already too late. The doctors told her that the baby was deformed and would die a painful death shortly after birth, if not before. They advised her to abort the baby. In spite of the way the child had been conceived, she did not want to lose the baby. At first she refused. But after a second doctor's opinion supported the first, she relented.

After the abortion, she went into a severe depression. She went back to using drugs and alcohol more heavily. Finally, deciding that she could not endure the pain any longer, she planned to take her own life.

She was visiting a friend in another state when she planned her suicide. She purchased a gun from a pawnshop, then began looking for the right place to die. She found a beautiful hill that overlooked a lake and set the date. When the day came she hid the gun in her purse, then asked her friend if she could borrow her van to visit some friends. As she began to pull out of the driveway her friend suddenly came out after her. She was carrying a book. It was *The Christmas Box*. She said, "Here, take this with you." The young woman thought it was an odd request, but threw it in the seat behind her and drove up to the lake. She parked, loaded the gun, then put its barrel in her mouth. She was about to pull the trigger when she heard a voice say, "Read the book."

She looked around to see who had spoken. There was nobody there. Then she looked back at the book. It seemed to have a faint glow about it. She set the gun down, got the book and began to read. She read it from beginning to end. When she finished she had a peaceful, warm feeling that she would see her baby again. That someday they would be reunited. She emptied the gun, then threw it into the lake.

She went on to write that she was still a drug addict, which is why she was in prison. But she was still glad to be alive, and it's because of *The Christmas Box*.

Dear Mr. Evans,

What a blessing!! I have been truly blessed by your story, The Christmas Box. *I sometimes read at night when I cannot sleep, and last night I started to read the story and could not stop until I finished. I had to stop several times at the end of the story to catch my breath because I was crying so hard.*

I am a single parent of a beautiful four-year-old girl. Lately the everyday stresses of my life have been bringing me down—being single and lonely and working full time. I have begun taking my frustrations out on my daughter. I have lost my patience quickly and have been snapping at her often. I have found myself feeling so guilty for getting upset and for yelling at her in a hurtful tone. I have been praying, asking God to help me.

Your story touched me and showed me that my daughter's childhood is so precious and that I have been given a gift in her. I want to cherish all the time I have with her. I want to love her as God loves us.

I am so grateful that you shared your family's story with others, especially with me! It made me look at myself and my own life.

Again, thank you and God bless you and your family,

Mary

◆

34

THE FLIGHT ATTENDANT

When we bury someone we love, we must also bury a part of our heart. But we should not bemoan this loss. Our hearts, perhaps, are all they can take with them.

THE LETTER

$\mathcal{I}$T WAS A FEW DAYS BE-
fore Thanksgiving and I was signing books at Joseph-Beth
Booksellers, a large bookstore in Cincinnati. The line was
long and my escort was getting anxious. "You're going to
have to hurry," she kept saying. "If you miss your flight
you'll never get home."

I finished signing and as I walked out to her car I had a
premonition to take a paperback copy of my book from
my suitcase and put it in my carry-on. I wondered why. I
had already read the book. I asked my escort to open the
trunk and I retrieved a copy.

An hour later I was on the plane headed home. When a
flight attendant asked me if I wanted something to drink, I
felt prompted to give her the book.

I didn't do it. It would be presumptuous, I thought, giving my book to a stranger. A while later she came back to
collect glasses and I again had the impression to give her
the book. As strong as the feeling was, again I resisted. But
this time I took the book from my bag and placed it in the

seat flap in front of me. I resolved that if she came back, I would give it to her. A few minutes later she walked directly up to me holding a flight roster.

"Am I supposed to do something with you?" she asked.

There was nothing mystical about her question. My publisher's travel agent had designated my seats "VIP," which did little but confuse the flight attendants.

"Are you referring to the VIP designation?" I asked.

"Yes."

"It means you're supposed to be extra nice to me."

She smiled. "I can do that. Now, why are you a VIP?"

"I'm not," I replied. "I'm an author. I'm on book tour."

"Would I know anything you've written?"

"I've only written one book." I lifted the copy from the pocket in front of me. "Have you ever heard of *The Christmas Box?*"

She looked at it. "No. Is it a children's book?"

"It's an adult Christmas story. Would you like a copy?"

"Sure. Thanks."

I handed her the book and she went back to her station. *That was fun,* I thought sardonically.

About a half hour later I noticed a different flight attendant making her way from the back of the plane. She was young, with dark skin and black hair that fell down across her shoulders. When she got to my seat she stopped. "Excuse me, are you Mr. Evans?"

I looked up at her. "Yes."

She moved closer to me. "Did you write a book that helps people who have lost babies?"

I noticed that tears were welling up in her eyes. "Yes," I said.

"My baby died." She knelt next to my seat and began to cry. I put my arms around her, ignoring the other passengers in first class, who watched curiously. Then she said, "A few days ago I got this newsletter from a grief support group I joined. It said that they recommend we read your book. It made me angry. I didn't want to read a book. I just wanted my baby back. I said to God, 'Why have you done this to me? Where are you? If you really care, please let me know. Please give me a sign that you care.'" Then she looked me in the eyes. "He sent you."

I talked to her for a while longer, then the pilot came over the jet's PA announcing our approach. She stood to go, hugged me, then said, "Thank you for coming."

35

◆

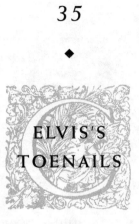

ELVIS'S
TOENAILS

Those who take themselves too seriously are the greatest jesters of all.

RICHARD PAUL EVANS

$\mathcal{N}$OT ALL OF MY EXPERIences at that time were spiritual. Some were just strange. Probably the most peculiar experience I had occurred in Atlanta. I had arrived for a live interview on *Good Day Atlanta* when I was told that my interview was not today but tomorrow. They apologized for the misunderstanding, but as I was still in town, it was not a problem and we rescheduled my appearance. The next day we returned to the studio.

As I was preparing to go on, the man connecting my microphone said, "Do you know why you were bumped yesterday?"

I said, "I was told that there was a scheduling mix-up."

"No, you were bumped," he said. He grinned wryly. "Do you want to know why?"

"I guess."

"Some woman came on. She was Elvis's pedicurist or something. She had Elvis's toenails."

"Elvis's toenails?"

"They were in a little jar."

"I was bumped for a jar of Elvis's toenails?"

He switched on my microphone and smiled. "You sure were. Have a good show."

36

◆

THE TOP

There comes to each life at least one Betheltown.
But it comes only once and we dare not ask for more.

THE LOCKET

$\mathcal{T}$WO DAYS AFTER THANKS-
giving I left on the road again. That same week I arrived in
New York for another appearance on the *Today* show. My
segment followed Martha Stewart's. I was again interviewed by Katie. She asked how our new baby was. I was
amazed that she remembered or cared enough to ask.

Simon & Schuster had set up a toast to celebrate the
success of my book. Not five minutes into the party my
publicist walked into the conference room. "I have an an-
nouncement," she shouted above the din. "I just got off the
phone with *USA Today. The Christmas Box* just passed
Howard Stern on their list. *The Christmas Box* is now the
number-one book in America!"

◆

A few days later I returned to Salt Lake City for the December 6 angel ceremony. Utah's KTVX television had

come down to my office to interview me before the event when they learned that I was waiting for the advance report from the *New York Times*. Their camera was on me when I learned that I had hit number one on the list.

37

◆

ANOTHER SIGNING

*I have learned much about loss from their pain.
Oftentimes it takes the darkness of another's grief
to shed light on our own.*

THE LOOKING GLASS

$\mathcal{M}$Y LAST BOOK SIGNING of that remarkable year was at a Wal-Mart in West Valley City, just west of the Salt Lake valley. It was the last Saturday to shop before Christmas. By the time I arrived for the event, many in line had been waiting for more than two hours. I sat down at my table, rubbed my wrist, and began to sign. About a half hour into the signing a woman walked up outside the roped stanchions of the line and just stared at me. Then she shouted at me.

"I don't have time to wait in your line, Mr. Evans," she said.

The line quieted and those near the table turned to see who had created the disturbance. As I glanced up I noticed there was something dark and soulful about the woman's eyes.

"I just wanted you to know that my little girl was killed by a car last Thursday. I have read your book every day since then and it's the only thing that's keeping me going."

I walked around the table and embraced the woman as

she buried her head in my shoulder and wept. A few minutes later I returned to the table. The woman drifted off into the crowd. Those in line stood in stunned silence. After a moment a woman in line said, "I read that this happens at your book signings."

"Almost every one," I replied.

38

◆

A PROMISE
FULFILLED

$\mathcal{S}$HORTLY BEFORE CHRIST-
mas our family was in the living room with a photographer
from *USA Today*, taking pictures for the cover of the Life
section, when the phone rang. It was Mary Kay Lazarus,
my local publicist.

"We just received a phone call from the White House,"
she said. "You and Keri have been invited to meet the president."

About a week later Keri and I walked in through the
doors of the White House. The White House was beautifully adorned in its Christmas finery and we were taken upstairs to meet with the president's staff. After signing
books, we were asked if we would like to go down and
meet the president.

"Just like that?" I said.

The woman smiled. "Why not?"

She went down to check with President Clinton. A moment later she called up to us. "I'm sorry, Jesse Jackson just

arrived with his son. They'll be meeting for a while. But the president has invited you to be his guest in the presidential box tonight at the Kennedy Center. Then he'll meet with you in the morning after his radio broadcast."

We went to the Kennedy Center for a presentation of the *Messiah* and returned to the White House the next day, where we met with President Clinton in the Oval Office. As Keri spoke with President Clinton I could not help but be amused. Mrs. Clinton had just finished her book *It Takes a Village* and was about to go on book tour, and here was my wife talking with the president of the United States about what it was like to be married to an author.

That night, at a White House reception, Keri and I danced in the East Room to music played by the marine band.

"Can you believe this?" I asked Keri. "We're dancing in the White House."

◆

Since that time Keri and I have met actors, directors, authors, diplomats, political leaders, renowned journalists, religious leaders, athletes and sports legends, billionaires and business magnates.

We have eaten lunch at the home of President George and Mrs. Barbara Bush. I have shared the podium with

President George W. Bush and first lady Mrs. Laura Bush. I have visited with former British prime minister John Major and eaten breakfast with Elizabeth Dole.

My grandfather's words have come true. I have indeed walked with the royalty of this earth.

I have since considered that there might be another meaning to the words of the blessing. Perhaps what was meant in my grandfather's blessing by "royalty" was not, as I had always assumed, the powerful and famous of this world after all, but instead, the ordinary good people of this world who had endured the refiner's fire of loss and emerged as royal spirits.

Perhaps. I'd like to think so.

39

◆

DANCE

No little girl could stop the world to wait for me.

NATALIE MERCHANT, FROM THE SONG
"MY HOW YOU'VE GROWN"

$\mathcal{A}$ REPORTER ASKED ME why I had chosen a line from a Natalie Merchant song to use as an epigraph in *The Christmas Box.*

As appropriate as the words are to the book, I had an even more personal reason for its inclusion. One night I was playing with my daughters, Jenna and Allyson, when the song "My How You've Grown" came on the stereo. My daughters spontaneously began to dance, flinging their skinny little bodies about the room in rapturous motion. For the moment I was lost in the joy of that motion. As I listened to the words of the song, about the fleeting nature of childhood, and watched my little girls, I began to feel a little sentimental.

Allyson, who was only four at the time, suddenly asked, "Dad, what's wrong? There's water in your eyes."

I assured her that nothing was wrong, but she didn't believe me. She came over and sat in my lap. There was, after all, *water in my eyes.* I told her that listening to the song made me think about them growing up.

"Don't you want us to grow up?" she asked.

"That's a hard question," I said. I told her that I wanted her to grow up and have all the experiences life held for her. But I never wanted her to go away. And I never wanted this moment to end. She thought about it for a moment, then, with the music still playing in the background, she said, "Dad, then let's dance."

She got it right, I thought. Dance. Dance for the joy and breath of childhood. Dance for all children, including that child who is still somewhere entombed beneath the responsibility and skepticism of adulthood. Embrace the moment before it escapes from our grasp. For the only promise of childhood, of any childhood, is that it will someday end. And in the end, we must ask ourselves what we have given our children to take its place. And is it enough?

Dear Richard,

Though I am only ten years old this story touched me deeply. Now I know a mother's feelings when she says I love you. I have also learned why parents are so heartbroken when one of their children dies. Again, you touched me deeply.

Love,

Chelsea

P.S. I hope your family is touched too.

Epilogue

◆

*From our first infant babbling to our last word we make
but one statement, and that is our life.*
THE LETTER

Since *THE CHRISTMAS BOX's*
humble first printing of twenty copies, more than 7 million
copies of the book have been sold throughout the world.
Stacked atop one another they would roughly be the
height of 258 Empire State Buildings. Or about ten times
higher than Mount Everest. And the book continues to sell.

More important, the healing of the book continues.
Last year at an event in Cheyenne, Wyoming, a woman
with no more information than that I was somewhere in
the city had driven nearly two hours from another state to
find me. She wanted to tell me how *The Christmas Box* had
saved her daughter's life.

The woman told me that her daughter had fallen in
with the wrong crowd, spiraling off into a lifestyle that in-

cluded sex, abuse and depression. Her daughter developed an eating disorder and had starved her five-foot-five frame down to eighty-two pounds. In her daughter's own words, it was her way of committing suicide "without taking responsibility for a messy death."

The doctor warned the woman that her beautiful daughter was dying and as the girl resisted all help, there was little they could do but prepare for it. Then, one evening shortly before Christmas, the mother took her daughter shopping just to get her out of the house. While wandering through the store her daughter suddenly noticed a small book. She walked over and examined it. It was *The Christmas Box*. As she read its flap, she felt a powerful inexplainable urge to read the book.

Her mother bought it for her and that night she read the book from cover to cover. In a letter to me, the daughter described the experience as *a stream of light entering a darkened room*. For the first time in years she felt hope.

The young woman called her mother and told her how she felt about the book and asked if I had written anything else. Surprised by her daughter's sudden interest in reading, let alone anything, she went out and bought everything I had written. Her daughter said that through the process of reading the books she came to believe that God loves his children no matter how ugly the sin.

Since then she not only has recovered from her eating disorder but is now lecturing to other girls about the dangers of bulimia and anorexia. She has been a newscaster for a Christian radio station and a cheerleader for a national sports team.

The healing of the angel continues. In 1996 Utah's governor, Mike Leavitt, proclaimed December 6 Christmas Box Angel Day in Utah—a day of healing and remembrance for those who have lost children.

The angel statue is adorned, year-round, with flowers, candles, stuffed animals and notes to loved ones. I'm told that now and then tour buses wind their way through the cemetery.

Like the book, the angel itself is spreading throughout the world, as there are many who desire Christmas Box Angel statues for their own communities. The first request came from Elko, Nevada. Not long after, I received a call from the Oklahoma branch of the American Red Cross. They wanted an angel for the survivors of the Murrah Federal Building bombing. The angel currently resides in the museum across from the national memorial.

Reader's Digest chose the Christmas Box Angel as the cover story of their first edition of the century ("He Made Hope a Bestseller," January 2000). Millions of people around the world have read about the angel and the requests for angels come even faster now. As I write this, there are twenty-three angels and more than eighty more in the works. (For a complete listing of standing angels see the end of this book.)

The three Christmas Box House facilities that sprang from the book have already housed thousands of children. We achieved every benefit from the facility we hoped for—and many we hadn't anticipated. For the first time, large groups of siblings were kept together. Community donations to child advocacy increased 7,000 percent the first two months the Salt Lake shelter was open, and the average hours of schooling for a child in state custody rose from just two hours a week to thirty.

And we've just begun. Government leaders and child advocates from across America and around the world have toured our facility, and we are currently preparing to bring Christmas Box Houses to other states and countries. The Christmas Box House staff has addressed child advocacy world conferences in Budapest and Slovakia. Our organization was invited by the deputy minister of social services to consult with the People's Republic of China on child welfare practices. The day will come when hundreds of thousands of children will be served by Christmas Box House facilities and advocates.

Engaged as an advocate for abused children, I often see the worst of humanity. There is much evil in this world. History abounds in it. So does today's news. Still, through my journey and experiences I have become more hopeful of this world, not less. There is still more love than hate. We need to remember this.

There are those who will say that much of what I have

written about is no more than coincidence. Perhaps. Then again, perhaps coincidence is just God choosing to remain anonymous. I believe God's fingerprints are to be found all over the events of our lives. Decide for yourself. But if there is, in fact, a divine plan to make more of our lives, this is good news indeed.

The Bible says that "God hath chosen the foolish things of the world to confound the wise; and God hath chosen the weak things of the world to confound the things which are mighty." There could be no better explanation of the Christmas Box Miracle than this; through a small Christmas story, thousands, maybe millions of lives are somehow affected for the better. And if I cannot fully explain these miracles, it is of small concern to me. I'm satisfied just to be a part of it—a journey where the end, perhaps, was known from the beginning. The words of my grandfather's blessing have come to pass. But in the blessing there is also this warning and reminder: *The greatest work you will ever do will be as a father in your own home.*

When I step far enough from the trees to consider the forest, I wonder at the scope of the miracles wrought by this little book and I cannot help but marvel at my role in it and wonder, *Why me?* There are better writers and better people. Maybe I was just the only one listening when the story needed to be told. I intend to ask God, if I ever get the chance.

Current Christmas Box Angel Memorial Statues

◆

Salt Lake City, UT

Elko, NV

Pueblo, CO

St. Louis, MO

Evansville, IN

Bedford, TX

West Palm Beach, FL

Spanish Fork, UT

Oklahoma City, OK

Belleville, IL

Cheyenne, WY

Grand Forks, ND

Marco Island, FL

Wauconda, IL

Fayetteville, NC

San Jose, CA

Loveland, CO

Ogden, UT

Flat Rock, MI

Maple Grove, MN

Stow, OH

Rutland, VT

Westhampton, MA

This list changes frequently. For an updated list of angel statues and for information about the location of an angel in your area, please visit the Richard Paul Evans Web site at:

www.richardpaulevans.com
or call (801) 532-6267.

A Gift for My Readers

◆

Over the years, I have received many requests for a compilation of
material from my works—quotations, diary entries and thoughts
from the characters who populate my novels. I have used many of
those entries throughout this book.

I am pleased to now make available

THE QUOTABLE EVANS:
Diary Entries, Letters and Lessons from the Novels of
Richard Paul Evans

To order a free copy, please visit our Web site at:

www.richardpaulevans.com

or send your name and mailing address to:

Richard Paul Evans
P.O. Box 1416
Salt Lake City, UT 84110

Copies will be available as long as supplies last. There is no charge
for the booklet or the shipping and handling.

Thank you for your continued interest and support.

About the Author

◆

Richard Paul Evans is the bestselling author of *The Christmas Box* trilogy and *The Locket* trilogy, as well as the children's books *The Dance; The Christmas Candle*, which received the 1998 American Mothers' Book Award; *The Spyglass*, which received the Storytelling World Award; and *The Tower*. There are currently more than eleven million copies of his books in print. All proceeds from Evans's books for children go to the Christmas Box House International, an organization that he founded, dedicated to building shelters and providing services for abused children. He lives in Salt Lake City, Utah, with his wife, Keri, and their five children. He is currently working on his next book.

Please send correspondence to Richard Paul Evans at:

P.O. Box 1416
Salt Lake City, UT 84110

or visit his Web site at:

www.richardpaulevans.com

Richard Paul Evans is a nationally acclaimed speaker.
To request Mr. Evans for speaking engagements, please fax
your request to (801) 532-6358 or contact the above
address or Web site.